THE

O

OLD ENGLISH POTTER.

BY.

L. M. SOLON.

ILLUSTRATED BY THE AUTHOR.

NEW YORK:
D. APPLETON AND COMPANY,
1, 3, AND 5 BOND STREET.
1886.

THE ART

OF THE

OLD ENGLISH POTTER.

PREFACE.

IN the first edition of this work we thought it necessary to narrate at length how our curiosity and interest were, on our arrival in England, aroused by the discovery of two quaint pieces of Salt-glaze, seen one day on the window-sill of an old cottage in Staffordshire. How we devoted our leisure to the research of specimens of the various kinds of pottery made in the district, feeling, at every fresh find, our admiration increase for a ware which, to our astonishment, had so far escaped the notice of the Continental collectors, and how it was that we were drawn into sketching and etching some curious pieces of our collection for our own pleasure, and the gratification of some friends at a distance; a labour which ultimately led to the publication of the present work. These considerations would have been here out of place; the text, written principally to accompany and elucidate the etchings, has had to undergo some modification, as the examples with which we illustrate these pages are taken from various sources, instead of being selected from materials in our own possession; consequently, all that merely referred to these special pieces had to make room for remarks of a more general application.

Nevertheless, in venturing to reprint our incomplete essay, our plan will remain the same. We must repeat, in fairness to ourselves, that our ambition never went so far as to attempt a complete history of English pottery; our undertaking is limited to recording briefly the most important facts which mark the various stages of the early progress of the craft in England; the narration will occasionally be supplemented with such personal observations as have been suggested to us by the numerous specimens that have passed through our hands, or by the original documents given *in extenso* by the authors who have treated the subjects, and to whom we shall always refer the reader who wants to know more than he will find in our summary account. We shall also hazard, at times, some probable supposition, or simply point out a new ground for controversy, whenever puzzling examples and documents come to raise a doubtful point or present fresh problems for solution, leaving the question to be answered by more learned and accurate investigators.

The collection of Enoch Wood, of Burslem, was the first one, we believe, formed with the view of showing the progress of potting in Staffordshire from the seventeenth century, and it was dispersed after his death. However, one can form an idea of what it was from pieces scattered here and there in museums. Such a collection ought never to have left the Potteries. It was divided into four parts, which were sold for one hundred pounds each. One went to the South Kensington Museum; the others were bought by the Jermyn Street Museum, the Mechanics' Institution at Hanley, and Mr. Herbert Minton, who presented his share to Stoke Museum. We must also mention that in his lifetime Enoch Wood sent one hundred and twenty pieces to the King of Saxony.

Brought together as they were, his specimens forcibly exemplified what genuine old English art had been in its pristine days, and one could have derived from them the knowledge that can hardly be gathered now from the stray and rare bits which have come down to us, unclassed and disregarded. The formation of a collection similar to what Enoch Wood's must have been, became the goal that we strove to reach, as soon as, under much altered circumstances, we began our researches for early and typical examples of English ware. The description of the specimens which should be selected to constitute an ideal collection of the sort, will form the subject of the following pages. It is to be lamented that the early pieces, showing the skill of the first potters, mostly made for daily use, have shared the doom of all common things, and now broken and destroyed, have disappeared almost completely. It seems as though the English people, whose genius revels in an ever-renewed manifestation of power, whilst hastening to produce a new manufacture, had done their best to make away with all that recalled a beginning of which their present glory made them somewhat ashamed.

And yet is there anything more interesting for an inquisitive mind than to trace back the progress of an art to its remotest sources; to follow the wandering attempts of its infancy, timid and unexperimented, but charming for us, because we are always charmed by all that is young? Nothing is to be found there but what is original and sincere, nothing that looks borrowed from conventional rules, misunderstood and ill-applied.

The Greek artist, who by a geometrical tracery originated the symbolical figure of a wave, and placed it at the bottom of a wall or at the foot of a vase, was a creator and a poet; he who came next, and understanding the purport of the work of his predecessor, definitely settled the best use to which it could be put, may be termed a skilful and learned man; but what can we say of the reckless imitator, who, coming at a later period, employs indiscriminately the most commonplace designs of the past, distributing at random figures and ornaments, all dead letters to him, upon any surface, with the sole view of making it gorgeous, and (to take one example out of a thousand) will uncoil the symbolic wave of the Greek on the border of a fire-stove? Nothing of the kind is to be found on the works of the potters we propose to study; and we must confess it is chiefly from abhorrence of these out-of-place decorations, often the fruit of a too hasty revival, that we feel attracted towards primitive works, always sound, fresh, and rational. Saturated with sophisticated embellishments, pursued everywhere by ornaments spread on every available space, whether wanted or not, we like to rest our eyes and our mind in looking sympathetically upon the simple attempts of the earliest ceramic artists.

When we began hunting and collecting old English Pottery we felt like a traveller traversing a country as yet unexplored, who meets with a fresh discovery at every step; and the reader will understand the deep interest we took in studying those specimens of an art completely unknown to us. The huge Slip-decorated dish, ornamented with the stately figures of King and Queen, or rather the abstract conception of what royalty might be. Exceptional and proud production of one of the common potters of Staffordshire, trying his hand at art for the first time, which, highly prized in its day, never left the dresser it was made to adorn but on the grand festive days, when it was used to bake the fat goose. The cradle of coarse clay, made on the occasion of the great-grandmother's christening day, and brought on the table for the first time two hundred years before, filled with filberts and walnuts. The traditional tyg, embellished with an unlimited number of handles, and bearing in large letters the name of its possessor. The capacious posset-pot, wherein the compound liquor was brewed at Christmastide only. The lucky shoe, a wedding present, the hob nails of which, made of white slip dots, formed under the sole the name of the owner. The four-handled candlestick, an ornamental article, preserved on the mantel-shelf, together with the most curious belongings of the family, and not the less admired for never being used. The white and delicate Salt-glaze ware, stamped or embossed all over with characteristic ornaments. The highly-glazed and richly-coloured tortoiseshell pieces. The Agate-ware, formed of variegated bodies, harmoniously blended. The cream-colour, so quickly attaining a perfection that has never been surpassed. All these, and a host of other varieties, were equally exciting our admiration, for in all of them we could unmistakably trace that freshness of feeling which is so often wanting in the productions of a more refined epoch.

In this way we shall endeavour to pursue our principal object, which is to relate, as far as it is in our power, the efforts and trials of the first plodders in the field, the unknown ones, who can have no special history of their own, but who, working as a group, made the ground ready for the splendid achievements of the great potters of the latter part of the eighteenth century.

The discoverers of the early hour are doomed to be absorbed into the commanding individuality of the man who, at the appointed time, arises to condense all their ideas. Setting into shape all that was still rudimentary and unconnected, he appropriates to a definite use all the various processes which, up to his time, had been little more than so many experiments, and settles the practical rules with which his name will be for ever associated. This is how it happens that the fame of the pioneers of the art is eclipsed; their work remains anonymous, and no one cares any more for the names of the forgotten ones, whose combined exertions had such an important share in bringing their craft nearer to perfection. Yet history, which repeats itself, often shows that as long as these early and active labourers are toiling, each of them brings a fresh stone to the edifice; but as soon as the great man, the practical genius, makes his appearance, he seems to erect in the path an insurmountable barrier; he marks the limit, and no one will ever go further. Like the fruit which completes the growth of some of the Eastern plants, he is the sure sign of the coming end; after the fruit has ripened, the plant slowly withers and dies. Retracing the steps of the deviated tradition, to start again from the source will always have a charm for the artist, if, by assiduously studying the works of the unknown and the forgotten precursors, he may gather something for which credit may, however tardily, be given where it is due.

This is why we do not intend setting before our readers any specimens of a later date than the middle of the eighteenth century. The several types it is our purpose to describe are not sufficiently numerous or varied in their manufacture to require a scientific classification; neither is a chronological arrangement called for, seeing that they are all comprised within the short period of one hundred and fifty years. In the same way as they are grouped on the shelves of our own collection, we ask permission to present them hereafter. We shall classify them under the following headings:—

Early Pottery—A short retrospective account

of the ware which was produced in England before the seventeenth century.

THE STONE-WARE—Which in the South of England was one of the first attempts at improvement made by the potters, in order to supply the goods hitherto imported from Germany. This object being at last successfully achieved by *Dwight*.

SLIP-DECORATED WARE—Or pieces made of the rough marl from the coal measures, ornamented with diluted clay, poured in cursive tracery on the surface, and glazed with "galena."

THE DELFT-WARE—Made in imitation of the Dutch importations; too good an imitation perhaps, as it can hardly be distinguished from the foreign productions, but which, nevertheless, cannot be overlooked, because of its having been extensively manufactured in many parts of England.

THE SIGILLATED OR STAMPED WARE—A process probably derived from the German Stone-ware, but which had become thoroughly English when the successors of the *Elers* began to employ clays of different colours, glazing them with "lead ore."

THE SALT-GLAZE—White and delicately-made Stone-ware, the most English of all in its characteristics, decorated with sharp and quaint embossments, or (but only at a later period) with enamels, and even with printing.

THE TORTOISESHELL—Rich and harmonious,

with underglaze colours, similar in effect to the works of *Palissy*, and of the early potters of the Continent, but differing much from them by the style of the shapes and decorations; and, lastly:

THE CREAM-COLOUR—Beginning with the discovery of the use of flint by *Astbury;* the first step towards the white earthenware, which, brought by *Josiah Wedgwood* to the highest degree of perfection, was to supersede all others.

We shall close our account at the coming of the prince of English potters, to whose memory lasting monuments are not wanting—exhaustive books and complete collections. Moreover, his admirable works are so intimately linked to the modest productions of his predecessors, that to write about them is in a manner to make an introduction to the study of his achievements, and indirectly to pay homage to his genius.

From a visit to the collection which Mr. H. Willett has so generously lent to the town of Brighton, a great amount of information can be derived; nowhere are to be seen so many striking and valuable testimonies to the art of our early potters. A few collectors of taste have not thought it unworthy of their pursuit to secure fine representative examples of the old English earthenware, and it is a piece of real good fortune to be permitted to admire the choice selections possessed by Dr. Diamond,

Professor Church, Mr. Soden Smith, and many others; and above all, the admirable collection formed by Lady Charlotte Schreiber, by her lately presented to the Museum of South Kensington. There is also no lack of interesting pieces to be seen in the public museums, though perhaps justice has not altogether been done there to the productions of the British potter; his little show, selected without much discrimination, and carelessly arranged, stands a poor chance of looking creditable amid the gorgeous display of foreign faïence by which it is surrounded. We must, however, make an exception in favour of Jermyn Street Museum, which, with its admirable catalogue, forms of itself a complete study.

Before concluding these introductory remarks, it is our duty to cordially thank those to whom we are indebted for assistance in the completion of this book. We stand under so many obligations, and our debt of gratitude is so heavy, that we are at a loss to know whom to thank most; we had better confess at once that if there is any interest in what will be found hereafter, the credit is due to others. The greater part of our information we have borrowed from the works of such painstaking explorers in the way of ceramic history as Marryat, Chaffers, Miss Meteyard, Mr. Jewitt, and many others. We need not mention their books, for they are so well known. For the formation of our collection, we are indebted to the generosity and unremitting exertions of so many kind friends, that we cannot attempt to thank them separately for the possession of the fine specimens which, through their kindness, have passed into our hands.

Last, but not least, we have to acknowledge thankfully the valued assistance received from our old friend, Basil Holmes, the painter, and from Mr. J. L. Cherry, of Stafford, who both kindly undertook the revision of these pages; and although we have still to beg that allowances may be made for the shortcomings of a foreigner, we feel less diffident in presenting our incomplete sketch to the reader after it has so much benefited by their careful emendations.

STOKE-ON-TRENT.

CONTENTS.

Chapter I.

EARLY POTTERY.

Chapter II.

STONE-WARE.

CHAPTER V.

THE BROTHERS ELERS AND THE STAMPED WARE.

CHAPTER VI.

SALT-GLAZE.

CHAPTER VII.

EARTHENWARE: CREAM-COLOUR, AGATE-WARE, TORTOISESHELL, ETC.

Appendix.

FOREIGN IMITATIONS OF ENGLISH EARTHENWARE.

INDEX TO ILLUSTRATIONS.

CHAPTER I.

EARLY BRITISH POTTERY.

Pre-Historic Urns.—Roman Occupation.—Norman Period.—Mediæval Ware.—Conventual Pottery.—Common Ware of the Middle Ages.—German and Dutch Ware Imported.—Names of the Different Vessels, and their use in the Fourteenth Century.—Tudor and Elizabethan Ware.

EARLY BRITISH POTTERY.

THE opening of the barrows and grave-mounds scattered over the soil of Great Britain has yielded a large crop of urns and vessels of the pre-historic period, brought to light in exactly the same condition as they were in many centuries ago. The same explorations have also supplied a few implements of stone, bronze, or glass found associated with them. These are the only vestiges that can speak to us of the industry of the first tribes which inhabited the British Isles; they confirm the notion that the Ceramic is as ancient as any art practised by man, but they help very little to unravel the mystery of the epoch to which they belong.

While man is pursuing his onward progress through the periods which have been termed the age of stone, the age of bronze, and the age of iron, improving all the while his primitive handicrafts, pottery alone seems to remain stationary, and alters little from what it was in the days when men first imagined how to fashion with their hands a lump of moist clay into a hollow receptacle. In the Saxon barrows, amongst weapons cleverly wrought, elegant phials of glass, and delicately chased ornaments of gold and silver, which, by the skill that they display, do not speak of a very remote antiquity, are found clumsy urns and cups of unbaked clay, which in no way differ from those that we may have reason to consider as being of some centuries earlier in date. They bear no characters or inscriptions of any sort to assist the speculations of the archæologist, while the artist finds comparatively little of interest in their decoration. They have up to this time been classed under the convenient heading of "Pre-historic Pottery." Our wildest speculation may be far from realising the age of the oldest specimen; on the other hand, we know for certain that the tradition was kept up long after the Roman conquest. One was discovered on the banks of the Alan, in 1818, and was considered as having covered the ashes of Bronwen the fair, the daughter of Llyr Llediaith, the aunt of Caractacus, A.D. 50. But Dr. Birch, in recording this attribution, says that it rests only on probability. The clay with which they were formed, sometimes coarse and mixed with pebbles, but in other instances more finely prepared, has been taken as affording a possible clue to their respective ages. The shape, simple and rough, such as the hand of the maker can easily produce without the aid of any instrument, is incised or indented with diagonal lines, zig-zags, herring-bones, and punctures, or impressed horizontally by the application to the wet clay of

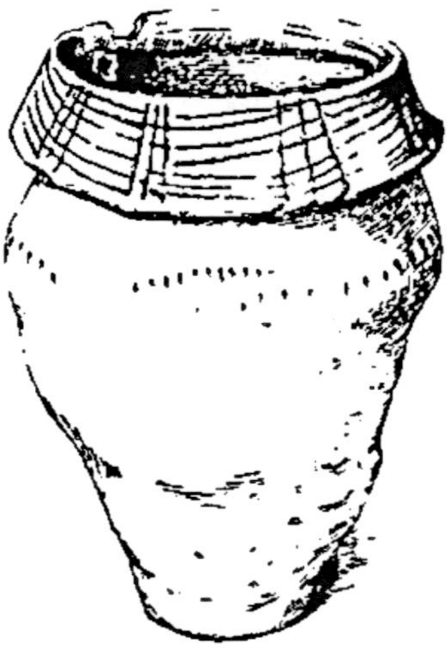

FIG. 1. EARLY BRITISH URN—LIVERPOOL MUSEUM.

twisted thongs or coarse ropes ; but whether termed cinerary urns, incense cups, or drinking vessels, they appear so similar in style that, owing probably to our imperfect education, it becomes a matter of great difficulty to point out any essential difference between the specimens discovered in the United Kingdom, France, or Germany. In some instances, an often reproduced form, or a certain disposition of incised lines adhered to in the simple patterns decorating the pottery found in the same locality, may draw us into the belief that these peculiarities constitute a style proper to the tribe which inhabited the soil; but if we lose traces of the same patterns upon the works of the neighbouring clan, it is only to find them again obviously reproduced on the discoveries made at a greater distance.

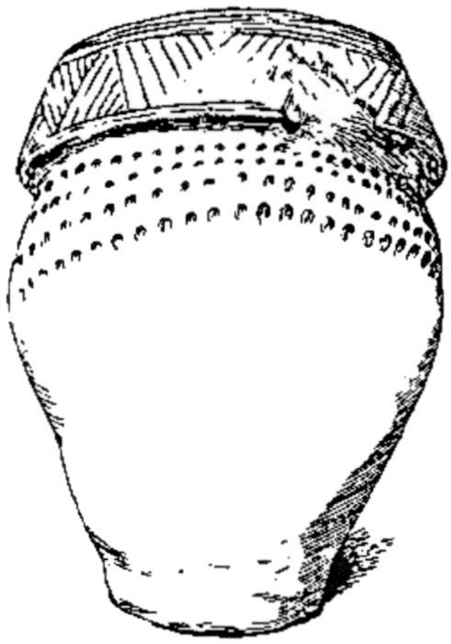

FIG. 2. EARLY BRITISH URN—LIVERPOOL MUSEUM.

So great a similarity exists between the fictile works of all primitive arts, whatever country they may come from, that the early Celtic productions recall, often very forcibly, the uncouth vessels kneaded and shaped by the women in the least civilised tribes of the new world. If a difference is to be noticed, it is not altogether to the credit of the early Britons' imagination. Most of the primitive races have seldom confined themselves to the mere geometrical designs contrived to embellish their first trials, but have generally attempted a rude reproduction of figures, animals, or natural objects; the barrows, on the contrary, contain nothing but the plainest shapes, hardly varied in character. During an indefinite succession of centuries the workmanship remains unchanged; even the instance of a rough ring on

FIG. 3. EARLY BRITISH DRINKING CUP—LIVERPOOL MUSEUM.

the side of an urn to serve the purpose of a handle, is considered as a remarkable occurrence. Sometimes made of well-beaten clay, they are only sun-dried; in other cases they are partially fired. Most of them were put on the funeral pile before being interred with the remains; by this act alone they were calcined; often the very soil where the cremation took place has been burnt to the consistency of brick. This being observed, must have led to the practice of firing some of the domestic vessels; but judging from the fire-cracks, and the inequality of the burning to be noticed upon almost every example, it is not probable that any kilns or ovens were ever used.

In Great Britain, votive vases are found in quantity, associated in the tumuli with human remains, whether cremation had or had not been resorted to. Their most usual shape is that of an urn with expanded mouth, having a thick band on the top, not turned on the wheel, but rounded by hand, and the surface ornamented with incised lines and punctures. The work does not exhibit traces of any tool but a sharpened bone or a rough iron point. From their supposed uses they have been arranged, according to their sizes and shapes, into four classes, viz.:—Cinerary urns, drinking cups, food vessels, and incense cups. The bones and ashes found in the first-named urns, or rather under them, since they are generally upturned over the remains, leave no doubt as to their employment; the three other classes may, perhaps, be said to have been named somewhat on speculation.

FIG. 4. EARLY BRITISH VESSEL.

At Trentham, at Stone, in Derbyshire, and all round the district now called "The Potteries," urns and vases of this class have been frequently found, and the modern potter can boast of being able to trace his ancestors very far back into past ages. Important collections have been formed of the ware of the early Britons, such as those of the late Mr. Bateman, Mr. Warne, and others. The British Museum, and the Mayer Museum at Liverpool, are very rich in curious specimens; their catalogues, and the works of Dr. Birch, Mr. L. Jewitt, Mr. J. B. Waring, and others, contain all the knowledge so far acquired on the subject.

Before the Roman occupation, as we learn from Strabo, the Phœnicians carried on an extensive trade in earthenware with the Cassiterides; so far no evidence has been adduced of the fact, which, if it be true, would show that the inhabitants of Great Britain were not satisfied with the products of their native industry.

From the first century to the fourth of our era, the Romans imported into the conquered country the most perfect processes and means used in the Empire; innumerable fragments of red lustrous, black, or light coloured ware, either plain or decorated, are unearthed from every place where they settled, yet they do

FIG. 5.
EARLY BRITISH VESSEL.

not seem to have imparted any of their skill to the aboriginal people.

It is only fair to observe here, that the red lustrous pottery so improperly named Samian ware, was never manufactured in Great Britain, but imported from Gaul, where the Romans were making it as well as in Italy. Most of the other kinds of pottery were certainly produced in the country, as has been ascertained by the discovery of several ovens and kilns. Those wares might have been imitated, their manufacture continued and improved by the natives; but, unlike the Gallo-Roman, who, by the side of his conqueror, produced an original style of pottery easily distinguishable, as is attested by the large collection preserved in the Museum of St. Germain, the Briton did not try to emulate the foreign master, and to add something of his own to an industry which was not calculated to answer any of his simple wants, so we can hardly trace any real British element in the Anglo-Roman ware, with perhaps an exception in the case of the Upchurch pottery, which appears to show some original characteristics, but there is nothing to tell whether that is due to the particular taste of the first native potter who worked there, or to any external influence.

To follow the transformation of this imported art, which, after having had for a long time a lingering and declining existence, at length revived and developed itself into genuine English pottery, would be too serious an undertaking to attempt here; but it may one day be made evident that one or more of the little pot-works, standing at present in some out-of-the-way spot, has never seen the fire of its kilns extinguished since it was occupied by a Roman potter. What we know for certain is, that the making of a coarse sort of ware has never been discontinued in England. Vessels of burnt clay are of prime necessity to all people, however low in many cases the level of civilisation; and their production is so closely connected with all the arts of fire, in the shape of melting-pots or crucibles for smelting metals and glass, and the making of bricks for ovens and other building purposes, that we do not require the discovery of earthen utensils, buried in the soil at different depths according to their age, to corroborate so indisputable a fact.

For us the question to be determined is, at what period did the use of earthen vessels become more general among all classes? Their improvement kept pace with the amelioration in manners and customs, the plasticity of their material rendering them peculiarly fit to fulfil the increasing requirements of a more refined society; but that it was only late that such a use began to spread extensively may be inferred from the fact of the craft remaining stationary for so long a time.

Of the Norman period we know but little; we

ask ourselves whether any discovery of importance would repay the trouble of searching for a style of pottery corresponding to the Norman style of architecture, or to any of the artistic handicrafts introduced by the conquerors amongst the Saxons. The manuscripts and tapestries of the epoch give some representations of the pots, basins, and platters then used, but there is nothing to tell us that they were made of clay. On the contrary, old documents mention most frequently drinking cups made of horn—material so generally used for that purpose, that in Anglo-Saxon an earthen pitcher is denominated a Tygle-Horn—glass, the making of which can be traced to a remote antiquity; metal, or ashwood; jugs of brass, pewter, or leather; and wooden trenchers. We must not forget that at the time of the Conquest the Normans were, like all the warlike people of the period, an essentially nomadic nation. Pottery was, indeed, ill suited to their roving propensities and wandering life; besides, they could hardly have brought into England an art almost forgotten in their own country; we know that such remnant of Roman tradition as still lingered in France had for centuries sunk lower and lower, and that until the revival of the thirteenth century, both countries could, as far as pottery is concerned, have found little to borrow from each other.

We must, rather than enter upon a long controversy, ignore two or three specimens, sometimes given as genuine, representative of the Norman style, and which are, in our estimation, of much more modern date. Our scanty knowledge of this period is, then, confined to coarse pots and fragments found in excavations. It is upon such unreliable examples that it has been thought possible to establish a parting line that would separate the Norman from the Saxon pottery; the imported one from the one that belonged to the soil. To affix a definite date to the precarious result of diggings, when nothing that is clearly proved and authenticated comes to support our speculation, is, to say the least, hazardous and liable to be easily contradicted.

Towards the middle ages fictile productions began to assume a more ambitious range. The floors of churches and convents were paved with tiles inlaid with clays of various colours, and whereon Gothic ornaments, and even subjects of figures were depicted. These tiles present a great variety of processes, being coated with glazes of different colours, embossed and pressed, stamped and sunk, inlaid or painted with white clay. Jugs like those preserved in the Scarborough and Salisbury Museums, and the one found at Lewes, are made in the shape of mounted knights wearing the costume of the twelfth century. By comparing these with the knights represented on the tiles of Chertsey Abbey, one might be led to suppose they also had a monastic origin. Tile-making was evidently introduced from Italy and France, where it was practised at a very early period by the monks themselves. Some travelling friars brought it over, and they were very jealous of keeping their professional secrets, applying them only to articles for their own use, whether tiles or such domestic earthenware as was required in the community. A very curious record is found in "*Nichols' Decorative Tiles:*" in 1210, the Abbot of Beaubec, in Normandy, was sentenced to "light penance" for having allowed a monk to work at his trade of a potter for persons outside the Cistercian order. With the making of tiles and other conventual pottery of the mediæval period, we find again the trade in foreign hands, and the same difficulty besets us to know what share the local potter may have had in the best productions of these times.

Far from entering the way to improvement opened by the monastic orders, we believe that the ware turned out by the common potter for homely uses was meanwhile becoming lower and lower in quality. It consisted of crocks of the commonest description, made with especial regard to cheapness; friable and brittle from being underfired to save fuel, and left porous and pervious. These wares were partially glazed on the outside with brilliantly-hued green, yellow, or brown, to make them look showy on the market place; yet we learn from the "*Liber Albus,*" that as early as 1271 it was ordered that "all earthenware should be well leaded." If ever the potter attempted an out-of-the-way piece whereon to display some unwonted invention, it was in the same way that a country baker occasionally makes a wedding cake. The consequence was that all articles made of clay were discredited, as being vulgar and unfit for any respectable person's use. Down to our own days we have kept something of that prejudice in the feeling of reprobation entertained against a clay pipe.

Only pots of one sort escaped the general contempt; these were the jugs and tankards of German Stone-ware, which were often expensively mounted in silver. More than once are they mentioned in the wills of the wealthy; but they were prized merely on account of their rarity, just as the Chinese collector, spoken of by a traveller, valued an English ginger-beer bottle which he had placed amongst his most precious porcelain. So different were they from all that was made in the country that they became an object of great curiosity. We should therefore be cautious before accepting any examples described in the old deeds as throwing any light upon the history of potting in England.

The names of the earthen vessels in use at the time were most of them derived from the French. They are:—

Cruske, Cruskyn, Cruche—A jug.

Crock—Also a jug, often mounted in silver or pewter.

Goddet or *Goddart*—A mug.

Gallipot—A small cup.

Botell, Flagon—A bottle.

Costeril or *Costeret*—A flask to be slung over the shoulder.

Many of these, coloured with mottled glazes, are evidently of French manufacture, and were, no doubt, brought over by travellers. Others in the shape of a bottle, marbled red and yellow, were of English make.

Jubbe?—Spoken of by Chaucer.

Just—Holding the exact measure.

Squel, Ecuelle—A shallow basin.

Pitchers—Jugs are still called pichets in Normandy.

Most of these pieces do not bear any décoration; yet the earliest, generally coated with green glaze, are heavily ornamented with embossed heads or rude foliage, the last trace of Roman tradition. At Lincoln, small moulds of terra-cotta were found, together with fragments of the fourteenth century; rude reliefs were pressed separately in these moulds before being applied to the ware. Last year two curious basins, ornamented all round with heads of the same style, were found at Chester; they were used as hand-warmers, and are precisely similar in shape to others dug up in Paris. The journals of the Antiquarian societies of England are filled with accounts of discoveries of this sort. We notice that articles ascribed to the middle ages are, as a rule, very coarse and common. They consist of jugs, pipkins, piggins, patens or bowls, watering pots, money boxes, children's toys—all articles made for the poor, for gardening, or for the most vulgar uses of the household. On the common yieldings of the excavations it is useless to linger, any more than upon the butter pots of Burslem or the garden tiles of Newcastle-under-Lyme, the latter especially not being very much above the bricks of the builder. Far from being, as they have sometimes been supposed to be, the beginning of a revival, we think that they must be considered as the fag-ends of an art fallen into disuse. Tygs, dishes, and pieces covered with a rich black glaze are not found amongst the former, being much later in date. These show no longer traces of moulding like the earliest ware; the knobs or handles are made by hand, impressed with the thumb or pinched with two fingers at the place where they join the body of the piece.

If we now come to the Tudor and Elizabethan period, we do not find that the records of the times, which allude to the introduction of earthen utensils amongst those in ordinary use, throw much light upon the particular share the English potter had in their making, nor to what extent he was assisting the development of his craft.

Chaffers ("*Marks and Monograms*," p. 52) quotes many interesting documents. From *Estienne Perlin, Paris*, 1558: "The English drink beer not out of glass, but from earthen pots, the cover and handles made of silver for the rich. The middle class mount them with tin. The poorer sort use beer pots made of wood." From *Harrisson*,

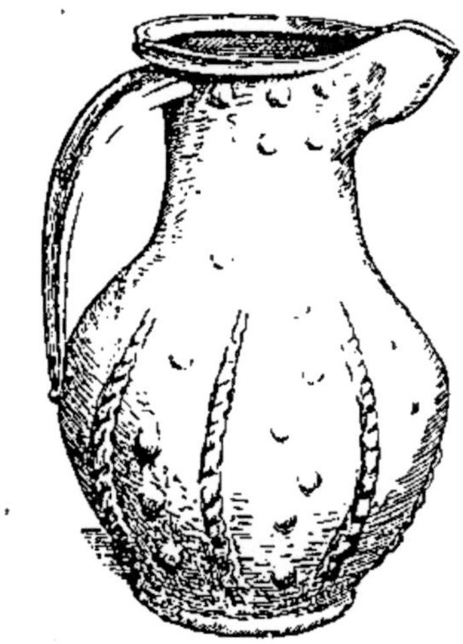

FIG. 6. GREEN GLAZE JUG.

1579: "As for drink, it is generally filled in pots of silver, also in fine Venice glasses of all forms, and for want of these elsewhere in *pots of earth*, of sundry colours and moulds, whereof many are garnished with silver, or at the leastwise with pewter."

But all the pots mounted with silver and pewter, if we may judge from the numerous examples that have come down to us, were no doubt of German or Dutch make. We do not know any instance of an indisputably genuine English jug or tankard associated with an Elizabethan garnish of metal, while there is a large number of foreign ones, the setting of which, whether of pewter or silver, is stamped with the English mark.

More to the point are the following quotations, also given by Chaffers :—From the books of the Drapers' Company, 1552, describing the election feast: "There were *green pots* of ale and wine with ashen cups before them." From the Losely MSS. in the sixteenth century: "The gentlemen of the Temple drank out of *green earthen pots* made from a white clay found at Farnham Park."

In the first edition of this work we have reproduced a puzzle-jug of our own collection, which bears the date 1591, the figures being thickly raised in clay. It is coated with the same green glaze peculiar to the mediæval English ware, which seems to answer the description quoted above. We shall ascribe to the same date a green pitcher decorated with horseshoes and buckles, the cognizance of the Ferrers, the Norman Earls of Derby, and which, on that account, has been by some authors described as a specimen of Norman pottery.

We must mention, but with a caution, the two brackets preserved in the British Museum. They bear amongst other devices the Tudor rose and the monogram of Queen Elizabeth, and are richly glazed with green and brown. They are considered of English make, but the style of ornamentation and the quality of the glaze remind one more of the Nuremberg stove slabs than of anything made in England at that time. One of them comes from Hampton Court, and we know that the decorative tiles of that palace were imported from Germany, therefore we feel somewhat doubtful whether these brackets might not have had the same origin.

Meanwhile, however, we find a few records of the importation abroad of earthenware manufactured in England. In the inventory of the collection formed by Florimond Robertet at the Chateau of Bury, dated 1532, we find the mention of some pieces of "fine pottery comming from Italy, Germany, & *England.*" M. H. Schuermans (Grès Flamands Limbourgeois & Liègeois) gives the text of a privilege granted to J. B. Chabotteau of the county of Namur, at the date of 1639, for the making of various sorts of earthen pots, in which we read this—"so far our country has been supplied with drinking pots, dishes, tobacco pipes, etc., manufactured in England & Holland"—unfortunately, of what particular kind was the ware here in question, has not yet been ascertained.

Nowhere do we find, during the times which correspond to the Italian and French Renaissance, the name of any potter who had attained to notoriety, nor does any nobleman of distinction appear to have shown in England a special interest in the progress of the art, by giving his patronage to any earthenware manufactory.

In Italy, *Maestro Giogrio* was everywhere acknowledged as a great artist, and kept at the Court of the Duke Della Rovere equal rank with painters and noblemen. In Germany, *Jacqueline de Baviere* made with her own hands the first pieces of Stone-ware. In France, *Helene*, Countess of *Hangest*, herself superintended the making of the wonderful Oiron Faïence. Later on, King Charles IX. and all his courtiers followed with the greatest curiosity the works of *Palissy*, and in 1606, Gonzague, Duke of Nevers and Prince of Mantua, stood godfather to the son of *Conrade*, "potter of Nevers," who is qualified "Noble homme," and his brother "Noble seigneur." Could we be surprised that the productions of the Old English Potter were of so little importance in comparison with what was done on the Continent, when we see how much he lacked encouragement? But times were getting near when he would readily answer the first earnest appeal made to his ingenuity and industry.

Towards the beginning of the seventeenth century, England seems to have awakened to a feeling of her inferiority, and we find the potter everywhere busy in trying all sorts of improvements, as will be seen in subsequent chapters. If the nobility did not yet require his earthen vessels, the people in their millions were demanding articles appropriate to newly-created wants; the gap between nobleman and commoner was filling up every day in consequence of the social changes which occurred in that century ; so between silver plate and rough crusking some gradation was steadily intervening. The man who with a little competence had also acquired a craving for better utensils in his household, could no longer put up with the coarse and plain ale pot of his forefathers ; when entertaining his gossip, he liked to see on his table some curious mug which should be a topic of conversation, perhaps an object of envy. With means and leisure came the desire to rival or excel his neighbour's luxuries. Colours and shapes began to be diversified, puzzle jugs of various combinations offered an amusement to the drinker unacquainted with the trick, and the marbled jug made in the shape of an owl became a subject of admiration to all. Tygs (like that in the Mayer collection, dated 1612), candlesticks, and posset pots were designed and potted by spirited artists in a masterly manner, that borrowed nothing from foreign notions. Instead of the dingy colours hitherto employed, the ware was made as white as possible with the Stone-ware body, or of the deepest black with the manganese glaze ; ornamentations of different coloured clays were sprigged on the ground, and appropriate inscriptions added a special interest to presentation pieces. From this sprang the several branches of English ceramic art, which we shall now try to follow up and study successively.

CHAPTER II.

STONE-WARE.

Stone-Ware and its Glaze.—Importations from Germany. —Mounting in Metal.—Stone-Ware made in England.—Early Patents.—John Dwight and his Discoveries.—Dwight's Porcelain.—The Fulham "Trouvaille."—Beer Bottles.—Francis Place's China.—Nottingham Ware.—Bear Jugs.

STONE-WARE.

THE body of Stone-ware is composed of plastic clay, to which is added some sand to prevent its cracking during the manipulation, and sometimes a small quantity of ground biscuit ware. Its hardness is due to the high degree of firing it has to undergo, which slightly vitrifies the substance all through; the glaze is a sub-silicate of soda, produced by throwing common sea salt into the oven when the heat has reached its climax, the fumes fixing upon the surface of the ware, and the soda being decomposed, under the action of watery vapours, by the silica of the paste. It is a hard, resisting ware, as its name implies, but not fit to stand any sudden change of temperature; it is very liable to crack or split if put upon the fire, or at the contact of boiling water. So in Germany, where its manufacture originated, it was confined to the making of beer jugs, tankards, or merely ornamental pieces.

So early as the beginning of the sixteenth century, many pieces of Stone-ware found their way into England from the manufactories established along the Rhine, escaping the almost prohibitory duties by being smuggled along the coasts. Mounted in precious metals, they excited much admiration, and, however rough and common, seem to have been treasured by their possessors. Most of them are of plain brown Stone-ware, with a granulated surface, but a few are of the elaborate white ware made at Siegburg. Some bear the royal arms, and for this reason have been mistaken for genuine English pieces, but in many instances the arms of some German town are blended with the former, which by this fact lose all importance as an indication of origin. The trade extended all over the country; even in Staffordshire common stone grey pots have been exhumed, mixed with early local pitchers, exactly similar to those found in the Rhenish provinces. We believe that there is hardly a town in England where there have not been found some of these bottles with a grotesque mask on the neck, that went by the name of "Bellarmine," or "Greybeard." Although some of them were afterwards made at Fulham, the greater number were certainly of foreign manufacture.

M. Van Bastelaer, in his work upon the "Grès

Cérames of Chatelet and Bouffioulx," says that the trade of those important centres of Stone-ware pottery rested in the hands of merchants, who made it their business to sell their productions in Flanders, and export them abroad. They contracted with one or more potters to buy all the ware they could make in the year, or for several years, and had it stamped with their own name or mark; to that class may belong the beer jug in the Widerberg collection at Christiania, which bears the inscription:

(WE) BARRETT IN HANDYARD IN HOLB(OR)N, LONDON, 1668.

Many of the specimens found in England so closely resemble those that are known to have been manufactured at the above-named places, that they may be safely supposed to have had the same origin.

The importation soon increased to such an extent that a certain *William Simpson* petitioned Queen Elizabeth, that "he may be granted the only license to provide transport for the drinking Stone pots made at Cologne, which had been so far imported by one *Garnet Tynes*, who is not one of Her Majesty's subjects."

The selling of these pots had become an important branch of home trade, and as early as 1534 the Pewterers' Company had obtained power to stamp their work in the same way as the goldsmiths and silversmiths stamped gold and silver plate. Early German jugs are frequently found with the English pewter mount, stamped inside the lid with the crowned Tudor rose. It is not, perhaps, useless to say, that as the pewter of England was considered the first in quality, the marks of the best pewter mounts made in Germany, bore also, in imitation of the English mark, a smaller rose, accompanied with the initials of the maker.

The great objection to earthenware had been in early times the porosity of such half-glazed pots as were then provided for common use, and their liability to break when roughly handled. The Stone-ware had neither of these defects; and here again the practical turn of the British spirit is evinced by the readiness with which people of all classes in England appreciated and patronised the hard, resisting ware of Germany, as soon as it made its appearance in this country. The merchants would never have thought of importing the gaudily-enamelled Faïence of Italy or France, and no one among the early English potters would have been tempted to imitate it; but all could understand the qualities of a new ware so well adapted to their requirements; so, while the merchants were bringing over from the banks of the Rhine large supplies of Stone pots, the first efforts of the potters were directed towards finding a home-made substitute that would take the place of a foreign article so much in demand. It may be that the first factories of Stone-ware were carried on in England with the assistance of workmen brought over from Germany or the low countries; the trade between England and the continent was increasing every day. As German and Dutch potters were commonly coming over to buy clays and raw materials, it is probable that the facilities the English soil afforded for an enterprise of the kind may have struck them more than once, and induced some to settle here; but at the same time several patents were granted which prove that the national potter did not mean to leave the trade in foreign hands.

William Simpson, above mentioned, after having asked for the sole license to bring Stone pots into the realm, promises that, "in him lieth the power of making such like pottes into some decayed town," but whether he carried it into effect is not known.

In 1626, a patent was granted to *Thomas Rous & Abraham Cullen*, of London, merchant, "Whereas,—heretofore & at the present time, this our Kingdome of England & other our dominions, have been served with Stone pottes, Stone jugges, Stone bottelles, out of foreing parts from beyond the seas," a patent was granted to *Rous & Cullen* for having discovered "the art of making Stone pottes," &c., "never formerly used in our Kingdome of England." We may perhaps remark here that, although the latter of these two potters describes himself as being of London, his name seems to imply that he, or at least his family, were hailing from Cologne.

In 1636, a patent was granted to *David Ramsey, Esquire,* and others, for, amongst other inventions, "the making of Stone jugs, bottelles, and which now are made by strangers in foreing parts."

In 1671, a patent was also granted to *John Dwight,* "for having discovered the mistery and inventions of the Cologne ware," and also "that he designs to introduce a manufactory of the same ware into our kingdom of England, where they have not hitherto been wrought or made." To this we shall hereafter more fully refer.

Mr. Jewitt *(Ceramic Art of Great Britain)* gives the full text of these interesting patents. We cannot help being struck by the way in which each ignores the previous ones, and we fear that great reliance cannot be placed upon records of inventions that have left so little trace. In the first case it is not difficult to detect a pretence for claiming a sole license to sell the foreign ware, for which trade a monopoly had not yet been granted. We do not know what exactly to think of the others, but no pieces or "vouchers" that could safely be attributed to these men have ever been identified. As to *John Dwight,* we see that in 1671 he claimed for himself the invention of "the mistery of the Cologne ware;" we have more than sufficient proof that his works soon competed successfully with those of the foreigners, and even supplanted them in the London market; in fact, the Glass-Sellers' Company contracted with the inventor to buy only of "his English manufacture, and refuse the foreign." To him must be attributed the foundation of an important industry; by his unremitting researches and their practical application, he not only found the means of supplying in large quantities the daily wants of the people with an article superior to anything that had ever been known before, but besides, by the exercise of his refined taste and uncommon skill, he raised his craft to a high level; nothing among the masterpieces of Ceramic art of all other countries can excel the beauty of *Dwight's* brown Stoneware figures, either for design, modelling, or fineness of material.

We know that *John Dwight* established his manufactory at Fulham in 1671. The exact date of his birth has not been ascertained, but his biographers speak of him as having been educated at Oxford, where he was an M.A. of Christ Church, and as having been secretary to two bishops of Chester before he became a potter. Whether he modelled and decorated his works by his own hands is not known through any documents; but by calling any modeller to help him in this respect he would have departed from the custom of the trade of the period. As a rule, the masters then used to perform by themselves the most delicate and difficult parts of their handicraft. Like so many artistic innovators, he appears to have been jealous of his productions, and discontented with the small profit they brought him; at the end of his career he is said to have buried all tools, models, and moulds connected with figure-making, to prevent his descendants reproducing those figures after his death. In two little books now in the possession of Mr. T. C. Bailey, the present proprietor of the Fulham Works, are contained many recipes and memoranda written in *Dwight's* hand, with dates ranging from 1691 to the year 1695, and following. These are full of interest, but, unfortunately, the wording is often so obscure that little practical information can be derived from them; many of the terms have become obsolete, and besides, some of the mixtures mentioned may have reference as often to unsuccessful trials as to inventions actually accomplished.

For instance, these notes do not, in our opinion, throw any light upon the problematic transparent porcelain believed to have been produced by *Dwight*, on the strength of the specification of his patent. If we try to summarise the more likely recipes copied out of his two books, and study their various components, we find that in each case, whether it be "Stone clay for Gorges," "Transparent Porcelain or China clay," "Light Grey clay to endure boiling water," "Grey Porcelain by salt," or any other, we come to the conclusion that these compositions will merely make a good Stone-ware body.

In all cases the principal ingredients are the same; we find the "*best clay*," which is the plastic clay of Dorsetshire; the "*dark clay*," the same, probably, which is now called black clay, also coming from Dorsetshire; the "*white sand*," always used as a component of Stone-ware; and the "*fine white*," probably a sort of "*frit*," about the composition of which we are left in the dark, and which is made fine by being sifted through the often-mentioned Cyprus sieve. This fine white might be, if we knew more about it, said to be a mixture conducive to the production of an artificial porcelain, but not in any case if employed in the way specified in the book of recipes.

All the above materials are mixed in numerous combinations, and by altering the respective proportions of each the hardness of the paste is either increased or diminished. With them a good Stone-ware of a whitish or light grey colour could undoubtedly be obtained; but if we look at these mixtures as having any reference to the greatest invention with which *Dwight* has been credited by tradition, we must maintain that none of them can in any way produce a china body, or any other body which in the present acceptation of the word could be called porcelain.

Another explanation may perhaps be given about his invention; we may labour under a misconception of what could be considered, in *Dwight's* time, as a sufficient imitation of the Oriental porcelain to deserve having the same name applied to it. It may have been nothing more than the white Stone-ware, glazed with salt and highly fired; this is transparent in the thinnest parts, and we may assume that Salt-glazed ware was made so thin for the special purpose of showing some translucency. In *Dwight's* own words, reported by T. Houghton, we have a description of his china which indicates that a Stone-ware, and not a real porcelain body, was produced. Speaking about the Dorsetshire clay, *Dwight* says, "'Tis the same earth china ware is made of, and 'tis made not by lying long in the earth but in the fire." We need not insist upon the fact that porcelain, as we understand it, cannot be made with Dorsetshire clay. He lays great stress upon the high temperature to which his ovens had to be brought, hoping to succeed by a greater fusibility; but while making all sorts of experiments, the probability is that he continued to manufacture his white Stone-ware, trying to make it transparent by casting it thin and firing it hard. We are aware that most of his mixtures required a very high temperature; there is, for instance, in one of the books, a formula for a trial of a china glass (glaze) which could not be melted but at an exceptionally high degree of heat; but as, from the material with which it is composed, we do not think that this glaze could be suitable for any china body, this again affords another proof that the intended china was nothing like what we should now call by the name of porcelain.

We can see by the description of his successive trials how much *Dwight's* mind was engrossed by the desire of discovering the secret of the Oriental china; he mentions some specimens he had obtained of a new ware, very transparent, but so fusible that no upright pots and only flat pieces could be made with it. This leads us to surmise that his researches were engaged, like those of some of his contemporaries, in the deceptive track of producing porcelain by way of de-vitrifaction; that is to say, to try to impart opacity by excess of firing to a mixture transparent at its first degree of fusion; he shared the common mistake of his times, and he could not have succeeded any better than those who had in vain before prosecuted their experiments in following the same delusion.

Some years ago, the attention of collectors was directed to some small jugs of unknown manufacture and strange appearance. With their globular shape and their ribbed necks, they are so much like the stone pots made at Fulham that by some they were thought to be probably specimens of *Dwight's* porcelain. The paste, somewhat resembling our modern parian, is very transparent, and covered with a good lead glaze. Mr. Willett has been fortunate enough to gather together several of these very rare pieces; they are all clumsily made, and most of them have the appearance of being mere trials; but a small mug of this ware is especially interesting, as showing an imperfect attempt at a coloured decoration, decidedly Old English in style, a fact which might weigh against the opinion of some collectors who attribute to them a Chinese origin.

The handle of another small jug now in our collection has been analysed by Professor Church, who found it contained nearly 5 per cent. of soda, a quantity very unusual in any other variety of china. To us it is very doubtful whether these pieces were ever made at Fulham; we do not attach any importance to the shape, which was imitated from German Stone-ware jugs; they may be the work of some unknown English potter, or perhaps essays made on the Continent. At all events, none of the recipes or materials set down in *Dwight's* two books could result in the production of a ware of that sort, and the "mistery of transparent earthenware" still remains a mystery.

The colouring oxides employed on the surface of his Stone-ware were cobalt and manganese, the purple and blue of the Grès de Flandres. The bodies were often tinted in the mass; the blue

Stone-ware was coloured with zaffre, the brown Stone with oxide of iron or ochre, and the Red Porcelain was made with Staffordshire clay, probably in imitation of that of the *Elers.* Sometimes the bodies were blended together so as to form a sort of grey and white marble, and then relieved by the application of ornaments made of white clay.

Had it not been for the Fulham "trouvaille" we should still be in the dark as to the precise characteristics of *Dwight's* ware. Twenty-eight pieces, which had been preserved in the family, passed in 1862 into the possession of Mr. Baylis, who at the time wrote an account of them in the "*Art Journal.*" Most of *Dwight's* different fabrics are there represented, yet not a single piece of porcelain was found amongst them; a few, like the white ware mug with Hogarth's "Midnight Conversation," the butter boat in the Chelsea style, and the pickle leaves, were either the works of his successors or purchases made from other potters and destined to serve as models.

But we are fully enlightened upon the merits of his Stone-ware by the admirable half-length figure (now preserved in the South Kensington Museum) of his infant daughter, Lydia Dwight, who died, as related by the inscription incised at the rear, March 3, 1672; she was modelled after her death, lying on a pillow (Fig. 6). We fancy we can trace the loving care of a bereaved father in the reproduction of the features, and the minute perfection with which the accessories, such as flowers and lace, are treated. A still more touching memento of the beloved child exists in Mr. Willett's collection; it is her little hand cast from nature, and reproduced in Stone-ware. Beautifully

FIG. 6.

STONEWARE FIGURE, BY JOHN DWIGHT, SOUTH KENSINGTON MUSEUM.

modelled also were the life-size busts of Charles II., James I., and their Queens, and a small figure of Cérés made of the same light-grey clay, now in the possession of the Rev. T. Staniforth. The mythologic figures, in imitation of bronze, were especially remarkable; the Jupiter of the Liverpool Museum and the Meleager (Fig. 7) of the British Museum, are worthy of an Italian artist of the Renaissance; the others, no less interesting, are unfortunately dispersed. Included in the same collection were also some fancy figures of a shepherdess, a sportsman, etc., a few marbled bottles of his Agate-ware, and a blue and white dish bearing the royal arms in the centre, said to have been one of a set made for Charles I.

FIG. 7. MELEAGER, BY DWIGHT, BRITISH MUSEUM.

Another find was made a few years ago, when, in pulling down some old buildings, the workmen came across a vaulted cellar, containing a lot of beer bottles and fragments of jugs painted with the blue and purple grounds generally seen on the Grès de Flandres; many were in the shape of Bellarmines or Grey-beards, having the grotesque head impressed on the neck; others were nearly of the same shape, but with plain neck, and stamped on the body with crests and badges, a crowned C (Fig. 8), Tudor roses, letters, figures of birds and animals, such as cocks and stags, these having reference probably to the inns for which they were manufactured.

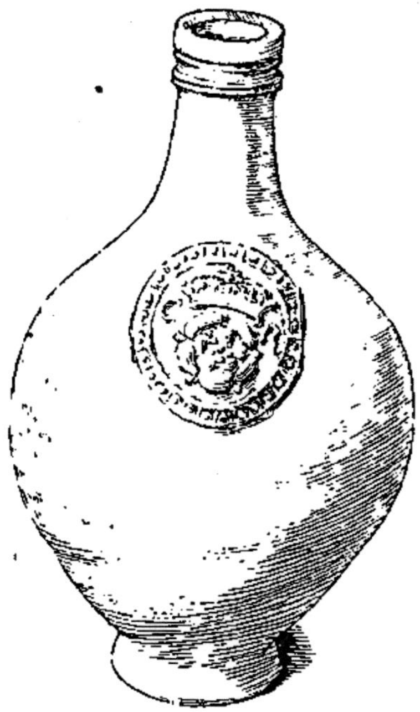

FIG. 8. DWIGHT STONE-WARE. COLL. L. S.

This makes the identification of genuine specimens very difficult, for these specimens are very similar to those imported from abroad ; both wares are of the same colour, shape, and material, and the decoration is identical, the larger portion bearing always the portraits or monograms of William and Mary, Queen Anne, George I., and George II.

For a long time after *Dwight's* death his descendants continued to manufacture the same sort of jugs and mugs. In cottages along the banks of the Thames have been found many large tankards, with the names of well-known public-houses. These tankards are of a particular brown Stone-ware, embossed with subjects that permit us to range them in the class of speaking pottery. Upon a large mug, evidently designed for a sportsman, are depicted graphic records of a hunting day: the flying game and the running dogs, the sun shining upon scattered trees, the huntsman himself mounted on his horse, and the inn where he stopped for a welcome rest. The picture was sometimes completed with an inscription incised in the clay. Thus we have seen the following lines on a mug of similar character: "*On Bansted down a hare Was found which led a smoking round. Abraham Hamman, Sussex,* 1725." Another mug in our collection is made of grey ware, partially coloured with brown. The decoration carries with it a political meaning. In the centre is a medallion of Queen Anne, supported by two beef-eaters, but the portrait was not sufficiently life-like to permit of dispensing with an inscription, and so we read round the top: "*Drink to the pious memory of good Queen Anne,* 1729." As the date is nineteen years after that of the death of the Queen, we may conjecture that the mug was made for an old servant proud of his loyalty to his late sovereign; the potter knew that nothing could please him more than a gift bearing such an inscription. One can realise the feeling of the old toper, when, drinking a convivial draught out of his favourite mug, he could take the opportunity to discourse with his friends about his past services, and what he remembered of the good old time. The pack of dogs is again running at the bottom; even on those made in our days there is hardly a piece of Stone-ware where they are not seen. Others, more frequently met with, have a coarse reproduction of Hogarth's "Midnight Conversation," in imitation of a Staffordshire Salt-glaze mug, a copy of which was found in the Fulham "trouvaille;" all these can safely be ascribed to the same manufacture. The history of the Fulham factory is related at length by Chaffers, and we learn that it remained in the hands of the family until 1862.

At the Manor House at York, *Francis Place* was experimenting upon clays towards the end of the seventeenth century; his trial pieces went by the name of porcelain. One of them is preserved in the Jermyn Street Museum; it is a small cup, neatly turned, of brown Stone-ware, streaked with black in the same manner as *Dwight's* Agate-ware, but highly glazed. Few other authenticated specimens, if any, are in existence, and the very name of *Place* would, no doubt, have been forgotten by this time, but for a few lines written by Horace Walpole in reference to the above-mentioned cup, which was in his possession, and so much treasured by him that he kept it enclosed, like a jewel, in a handsome leather case.

In the Staffordshire Potteries, about 1685, *Miles* and some other potters are said to have made Stone-ware; the probability is that they called by that name a rough sort of brown pottery smeared with lead. As salt-glazing was only introduced a few years afterwards by the *Elers*, the real article cannot have been manufactured before the beginning of the next century; at that time the making of the white Stone-ware, as we shall see in the chapter on Salt-glaze, became the staple trade of the country, and with it common utensils, as well as ornamental pieces, were produced in an enormous quantity.

The manufacture of brown Stone-ware became localised in the Midland counties between Nottingham, Chesterfield, and Derby, and so developed itself as almost to exclude every other common sort of earthenware. Pieces made in that district are easily distinguishable from those of Fulham; they affect particular shapes—loving cups, small straight mugs, puzzle jugs, and dark bears; the glaze is very smooth instead of being granulated, lustrous and metallic in appearance, and the decoration, instead of subjects in relief, consists mainly of scrolls, foliage, and flowers, scratched with a point in the wet clay before baking.

At Nottingham, crucibles for glass-makers were made at a very early period, and from this the potters were easily led to the making of Stone-ware. L. Jewitt describes the earliest example known; it is a posset pot dated 1700, made for S. Watkinson, the mayor of the town; it has all the features that characterise a ware which for two centuries has not undergone any alteration in style. The shape is thrown and turned, with

FIG. 9. NOTTINGHAM STONE-WARE. COLL. L. S.

handles made by hand; the inscription is in cursive characters, the flowers underneath are only incised in coarse lines, and the glaze is lustred by the remetallisation of the oxide of iron. Many other pieces are known, which are precisely similar as to clay and glaze; the scrolls, rosettes, and the conventional pink flowers are scratched with but little variation; the dates they bear widely differ, ranging from the earliest times down even to our own, and yet they all look as though they had been done by the same hand. We give here the sketch of a small jug of brown stone (Fig. 9), made with a double shell, the outer one being perforated with flowers and leaves, to make it look as if the body was pierced throughout. It belongs to the best period of manufacture, and is

FIG. 10. NOTTINGHAM STONE-WARE, NOTTINGHAM MUSEUM.

similar in size and design to the one preserved in the South Kensington Museum, which bears the date 1703. Besides these pieces, we may name the following: in the Bohn collection, a jug inscribed "John Smith, 1712;" in the Jermyn Street Museum, a punch bowl with "Old England for ever, 1750;" in the possession of Mr. Kidd, of Nottingham, a mug very elaborately decorated with roses and thistles, dated 1762; in the Nottingham Museum, a tall cylindrical mug, here represented (Fig. 10), upon which is inscribed, "J. & E. Holland, of Notts., made at Nottingham Feb. 16, 1781;" and "Why not this poor earthen vessel hold as precious a liquor as one made of gold?" and in our own collection, a puzzle jug of 1799. Neither these, nor the modern jugs and mugs, though ranging together over a period of nearly two hundred years, show any perceptible change either in manufacture or in decoration, and confirm what we have just said on the subject.

A curious speciality of the Stone-ware potters of the Midlands were the black bear jugs. We all remember the Bradwardine Bear in Sir Walter Scott's *Waverley;* it was a vessel peculiar in shape to the old English squire, as the glass or silver boot was to the German landgrave. Was not the good Briton readier for a laugh and a joke when he had emptied the comical head of the bear, whose uncouth body contained the foaming beer, than when his drink was poured out for him from a common-place jug of stiff and classical shape, at the sight of which he felt bound to assume a dignified and formal countenance? We must confess that they look rather grim and hideous; the body, coated with a very dark brown, is made rough by a sprinkling of small shavings of clay; eyes and teeth are of shining white paste; an iron chain is fastened to the collar, and a staff is fixed between the claws. Such as they were, in that time of bear-baiting they had a great sale, and were used either as tobacco jars or beer jugs ; the movable head in the latter case made a convenient cup. At Congleton, in Cheshire, nicknamed the bear's town, on account of the partiality of the inhabitants for those rough sports, they were in great demand, and large numbers of them have been found there, either of white or brown Stone-ware.

These bears were made at Nottingham, Chesterfield, and Brampton, where originated the making of those ponderous jugs and mugs with handles formed in the shape of a grey-hound, a pattern to which they still adhere in our days, and which is not going to be given up, if we may judge from the large quantity of them still turned out.

We must insist upon the difference that distinguishes the works of the factories just spoken of from those made at Fulham and the South of England. No doubt the grey and brown Stone-wares were first produced at the latter place, but thence the trade must soon have been carried to such locality as presented all the requisite materials wanted for this fabrication, viz.:—the proper sort of clay, and abundance of coals and salt. The Midland counties afforded all these commodities, and this was certainly known by all the potters of the South, and may have induced some of them to go and settle on such promising spots. Difficult though communication was in those days, there yet must have been a regular intercourse between potters working at a great distance from each other. We shall take only the instance of *Dwight* giving in his notebook the recipe for making the red teapots with Staffordshire clay, in the manner of the *Elers*, almost at the same time as the Dutchmen were producing them at Bradwell.

But in the Midland potteries the style of the Stone-ware underwent a thorough change; while in London the Stone pots continued for a long time to be made in imitation of foreign models, greybeards at first, and subsequently globular jugs with royal monograms, it was reserved for the uneducated workmen of these far-away counties to free their productions from alien reminiscences, and to create shapes and decorations which, plain and unpretending as they were, could yet without question be called their own.

The superiority of Stone-ware over every other sort of pottery for the uses of industry, either for utensils or for sanitary works, is so marked that its manufacture has always been on the increase, and the processes constantly improved; but little had been done to turn its merits into an artistic channel since the days of *Dwight*, until *Mr. H. Doulton* created the new style by which the Lambeth ware has become known and admired by the amateurs of Ceramic art all the world over.

CHAPTER III.

SLIP-DECORATED WARE.

The Slip Process.—Its Antiquity.—Its Introduction into England.—Localities where it was Practised.—The Staffordshire Potters.—A Pot Works in the Moorlands.—Dr. Plot's Account.—Reckoning.—Varieties of Shapes.—Names of some Slip Potters.—The Lettering and other sorts of Decoration.—A New Style of Slip Painting.—Richness of Colour.—Metal Mounts.—Inscriptions.—Modern Slip Ware.

Fig 11. Slip Dish—Wolverhampton Exhibition.

SLIP-DECORATED WARE.

THIS process, the simplest of all the means of polychrome decoration employed in early times, since it required nothing but the natural materials picked out of the earth, the Old English potter, in some sort, made his own by the diversity of effects he contrived to create out of it. It consisted in producing a design on the surface of the piece by pouring, through a small pipe, clay diluted with water to the consistency of a batter; this "slip" flowed in running traceries, or dropped in small dots, boldly contrasting with the colour of the ground. The Romans used it very cleverly, and many pieces are still preserved in museums, testifying to the skill with which it was handled. Graceful flowery stems are intermixed with running animals, stags and dogs, whose curved limbs are all produced by the same jet of slip, freely poured through the narrow spout of a vessel contrived to that end. Brongniard mentions the discovery at Lezoux (France) of one of these "pipettes," at the same place where fragments so decorated were found. That "pipette" presented at the lower aperture holes of different shapes, appropriated, no doubt, to the size of the intended design. A little vessel of almost the same shape was, for the same purpose, used in Staffordshire; to its spout quills of various calibre were fixed; when filled with

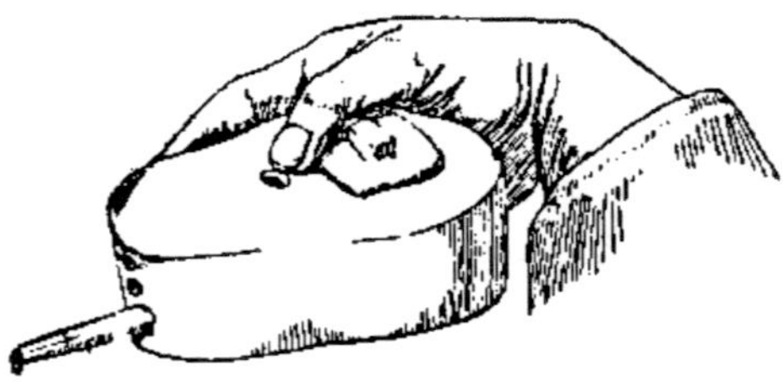

FIG. 12. POURING OUT THE SLIP.

diluted clay, the air was only admitted into the receptacle through a little hole pierced on the upper part, and the stopping of this hole with the thumb was sufficient to check the flow of the slip. In that way it was allowed to run unchecked to form the outline; dots were, on the contrary, produced by the intermittent admission of air. We give here a sketch which will complete our description (Fig. 12).

What connection there is between the Roman red ware, ornamented with trailings of white clay, and the oldest Slip-decorated English pieces, if, indeed, there is any, remains to be ascertained. Prior to the middle of the seventeenth century, we do not find any specimens that we could properly call decorated in that manner. The early tygs, made in the first part of that century,

FIG. 13. TYG, LIVERPOOL MUSEUM.

bear only applications of small pieces of yellow clay, which seem to have been pressed separately in moulds and stuck on. We shall give as an example the one preserved in the Liverpool Museum, which is dated 1612 (Fig. 13). Is there any connection between the English process and the one used in Switzerland and Germany? And was it through Wrotham, in Kent, that it may have passed into Staffordshire? Considering that examples made at Wrotham are somewhat earlier than the dated pieces of Staffordshire, so much might be surmised; but the truth is difficult to ascertain, as pieces undoubtedly anterior to what we possess in England are very scarce on the Continent.

Howbeit, at the date we speak of, we find this fabrication established in many counties. In Kent it was carried on at Sandwich, where a Dutch potter is known to have settled in 1582; and also at Wrotham, where very elaborate ware was made, including posset pots, dishes, candlesticks, and many different sorts of fanciful jugs and bottles. Although the earliest piece we know (a jug in the Maidstone Museum) refers us only to 1656, many others that can be ascribed to that locality seem by the style of the decoration to belong to an earlier period. Owing probably to the proximity of the Metropolis, the workman there shows a knowledge of the ornaments employed by the artist of the Renaissance on architectural sculptures, carved wood-work, the chasing of silver, and the patterns of embroidered cloths. The Fleur de Lys and the Pomegranate appear frequently. Dies, taken from metal work, began to be used for stamping on the decoration; we possess a terrine, or pie-dish, upon which many subjects of figures, reclining nymphs, and indescribable groups, are reproduced, borrowed evidently from the work of some facetious silversmith of the sixteenth century. These pieces are generally distinguishable from those we find in other districts by an overcrowded ornamentation. The handles on the posset pots are multiplied and covered with knobs, and all spaces between the principal subjects are filled in with a diaper of rosettes or stars. A stick, the end of which had been cut as a sort of rough seal, was used to impress the desired pattern in the moist clay, and the design is in some places coloured over with copper green, seldom, if ever, found on the old Staffordshire slip-ware.

Wrotham productions, generally of a highly ornamental style, were often inscribed with the name of the place, but little is known about the potters who worked there. Chaffers gives *Jull* as the name of one of them; and the site of his manufactory is known to have belonged to one *John Evelyn*, cousin to the author of "John Evelyn's Diary," to whom, perhaps, refers the monogram I. E., often recurring on tygs and other presentation pieces (Fig. 14). Antiquaries have as yet taken little trouble to gather documents concerning the productions of Wrotham, as has been done for the Staffordshire Potteries. It may be accounted for in this way, that the facts connected with a manufacture which was to disappear completely after so promising a start are less interesting to historians than those which refer to a district where the same industry slowly advanced year by year through a course of improvements until it had reached its present high state of excellence.

FIG. 14. WROTHAM WARE.

The manufacture was also carried on in Yorkshire, where, as the traditionary distich has it—

> "At Yearsley there was pancheons made,
> By Willie Wedgwood, that young blade."

In Cheshire, we may infer that the ware was manufactured extensively, from the fact of so many slip dishes having been discovered all over the county, and on the borders of North Wales. At the present time, indeed, at Buckley, a few miles from Chester, they have not discontinued the practice of the oldest style, and are turning out slip pieces which, with a little scratching and chipping, might be mistaken for the work of two hundred years ago. Tygs, of course, they are no longer, but the identical shapes now do duty for flower pots.

FIG. 15. EARLY TICKENHALL WARE.—COLL. L. S.

In Derbyshire, at *Tickenhall*, have been found interesting fragments of pottery, made of buff clay, occasionally streaked with brown slip; some of them, in the shape of roughly-formed heads, with head-gears and ruffs of the Elizabethan period, seem to indicate that they belong to the sixteenth century. The potters' field must have occupied at the time a very large area; since fragments have been found there upon ground extending over two miles in length (Fig. 15). Miss Lovell, of Calke Abbey, Derby, who has directed the excavations carried out on the site, has presented to the Jermyn Street Museum some curious tygs and bottles of this ware, selected from the collection she has herself been able to gather together. The place is mentioned as early as 1630 by Philip Kinder, and later on, in 1811, by Farey *(General View of Derbyshire)*, as being the centre of a very important manufacture of earthen utensils. The industry has now left the spot altogether. Slip-decoration followed there the impulse given in the Potteries, as is shown by the two authenticated Tickenhall dishes now in the possession of Mr. W. Bemrose. They are made of the usual buff clay, coated with dark brown, and decorated with subjects of dogs, trees, and flowers, traced in yellow slip. Many of the slip dishes, commonly known as Toft dishes, had probably the same origin.

But it was in Staffordshire that the slip process was to become almost a staple trade; there it may be more easily studied; there the old potter has left many records that will permit us to follow his progress. Was he himself the originator, or did he take the hint from one of those itinerant workmen who, at that period, used to begin life by travelling from place to place for a few years, learning a trifle here, and there imparting the small knowledge they had acquired in their travels? Who can tell? At all events, he soon created a style of his own, where imitation is not discernible. What did he care about the costly vessels then used by the nobleman and the wealthy? Himself one of the people, he made the ware of the people. Simple in his ways as his fathers had been before him, he worked out his steady improvements as a matter of course, and each step forward accomplished by one member of the craft, benefited the whole community. No patents were taken out, no secrets were kept, and from one end of the Staffordshire Potteries to the other all ovens turned out goods of the same description.

Miserable enough was the condition of the pot maker in Staffordshire, but the district afforded so many advantages for the production of earthenware, that it may be easily understood how it was that their number increased so rapidly. Clays and coal could be had by merely scratching the soil. The tilewright, a name given to the worker in clay whether he made tiles, butter pots, or crocks, was at no loss for his materials; and so, notwithstanding the sequestered situation of the locality, he soon commenced to improve his ware, and to find means of sending it away, first over the Midland Counties, and then to the very ends of the kingdom.

Miss Meteyard, in her life of *Wedgwood*, gives an interesting and forcible description of a pot work in the Moorlands in the seventeenth century. The oven—only one—was eight feet high and six feet wide. It was surrounded by a wall of broken saggers to keep the heat in, and this wall, later on, became the hovel. It stood in a secluded spot, most often at the crossing of two roads, near a little stream of water. Round the oven clustered the open sheds where the different operations necessary to complete each piece were performed, and the family dwelling, a small thatched cottage. The thrower worked in one place; the contrivance he used was of the simplest description, being rather a "whirler" than a potter's wheel. The potter's wheel is kept in rotation, while the hand that fashions the clay into shape remains fixed; the whirler differs from the wheel in this respect, that one hand turns it at intervals, bringing successively before the other hand the parts that have to be rounded. Next to the thrower sat the handler, sticking on the handles and spouts; what tools he used were certainly very primitive, being nothing more than a pointed bit of iron and a flattened strip of wood. In another shed were the man who traced upon the best pieces fanciful scrolls and lines of slip, and he who through a coarse cloth dusted upon them the pulverised *galena* for glazing. Very often the same man performed all these different tasks. Close by, the diluted clay was evaporated in the sun-pan, until it became thick enough to be conveniently worked, or else the moistened clay was thrown against a dry wall, from which, the water becoming evaporated, the lumps fell upon the ground, ready to be stored in a damp place for further use. Isolated from the rest of the world the potter worked there, attended by his sons and his wife. Sometimes a labourer or two completed the staff, which never seems to have numbered more than eight people. When the stock was ready for sale, the wife took it to the nearest fair, leading, pipe in mouth, the double-panniered asses, and there either sold her goods to the cratemen, or exchanged them at the town shops for such articles as she wanted to take back home.

In his History of Staffordshire, published in 1686, Plot gives a valuable account of the manufacture of pottery at that period. The complete quotation has been given many times, so we shall only recall here its principal features.

Many sorts of clays had already, as we may see, been experimented upon, and their different uses settled, as well as their mixing. Four different kinds were called "throwing" clays, and were used to form the bodies of the vessels. These were the *Bottle-clay* and the *White-clay*, of which the light-coloured ware was made (this was always of a dull yellow colour, for, light as the clay was, the glaze gave it a deep tint); the *Hard Fire* and *Red Blending-clay*, .which, mixed together, produced a black ware. Of more pliable nature, and used only for decorative purposes, "to paint with," were the *Orange*, the *White*, and the *Red Slips*, the last named of which, when mixed with manganese, turned black under the glaze. All these are easily distinguishable on the works of that period.

The author goes on to tell how the clay was mixed with water in a tank, cleansed from all gravel and other foreign particles, then beaten with a bat, and brought on to the wheel "to be formed as the workmen sees good;" all processes which do not differ much from those practised in our own time. The ware when dry was "slipped or painted." The orange slip made the ground of the ornaments, while the outlines were traced with the dark red slip, studded over with small white dots. In some instances, broad stripes of red and yellow, while still wet, were mixed together with a wire brush, which acted like the comb used for marbling paper or graining wood. Manganese appears to have been the only metallic oxide employed; it was mixed with lead, and "called *magnus* by the workmen." It produced the *motley colour*. As a rule the glaze consisted of the *lead ore (sulphuret of lead)* from the Derbyshire mines, in its native state. When a higher *gloss* was required, lead calcined into powder was dusted over the pieces.

The peculiar way of reckoning the ware ends

the description. A unit is said to have been represented by a dozen small pieces, and that unit served as a basis of reckoning for all the rest. For instance, a dish might have been worth a dozen ; a very large dish counted for two dozens ; of bowls, jugs, cups, and other articles of middle sizes, it required two, three, or four to make a dozen, and so on for all. In that way the potter knew at once the value of the contents of his oven by the number of dozens put in, while the workman could easily calculate his wages by the number of dozens he made in the week. Besides, in the event of any alteration in the prices of the ware having to be made, the unit alone had to be altered, and the scale was modified in all its items. So convenient was this mode of reckoning that, strange as it may appear, it has been kept up to this day in many manufactories, both in England and on the Continent.

Among the Slip-decorated pieces which have come down to us, we often find replicas, the shapes being neither numerous nor varied. The potter keeps to a few simple types, all Geometrical in their outlines ; but these he endlessly varies by decoration painted on the surface, departing in that manner from the taste of his predecessors, who, still under the influence of Gothic art, affected to indulge in modelling natural forms : the representation of a man, or of some heraldic animal. If we find little variety in the shapes of this particular ware, it may be accounted for by the simplicity of the tools employed, with which nothing more complicated could have been made, and also by the destination of the pieces, which were all intended for mere domestic purposes; and even such exceptional productions as the workman destined for a handsome present, were only made finer and richer by an additional display of slip-painting.

We shall now mention briefly the different descriptions of earthen utensils most in use at that time; there were: the *Dish*, which we still find in large numbers, and in every variety of size and ornamentation. The *Tyg*, a tall cup, the simple outline of which was enriched by an unlimited number of handles, always diversified by the fancy of the maker. The *Piggin*, often finely decorated; this is a small and shallow vessel, provided with a long handle at one side for the purpose of ladling out the liquor brewed in the tyg. The *Candlestick* (Fig. 16), found most frequently in the south of England, and often adorned, like the tyg, with numerous handles. The *Cradle;* these, on the contrary, being almost peculiar to the Midland counties, are seldom found elsewhere. The *Jug*, including such fanciful pieces as Bears and Owls, and also the *Puzzle Jugs*, on which the number and position of the nozzles show innumerable varieties of combinations. If we add to these a few specimens of very scarce

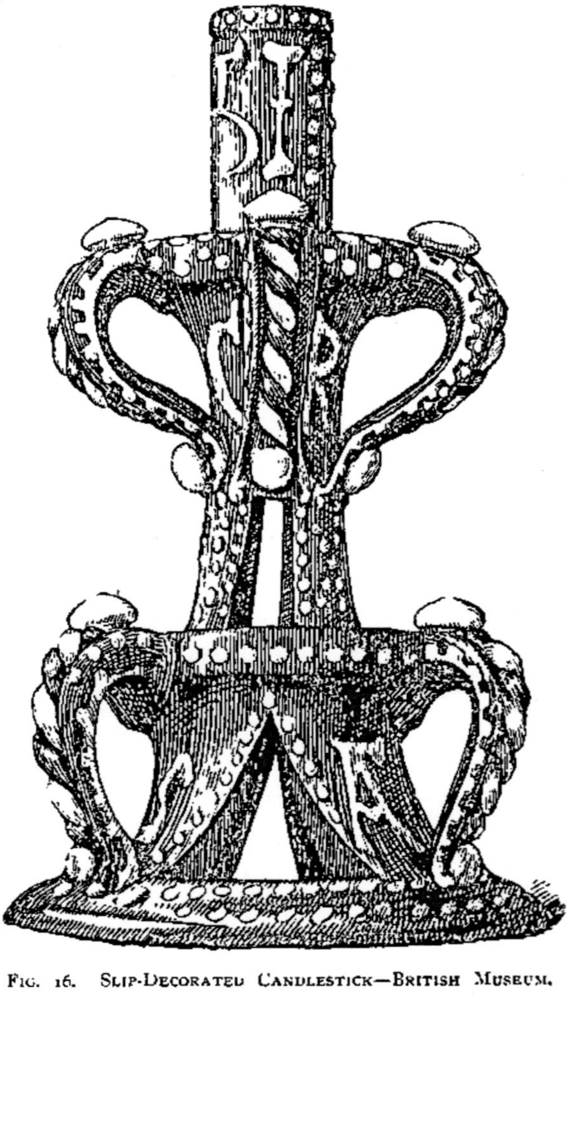

FIG. 16. SLIP-DECORATED CANDLESTICK—BRITISH MUSEUM.

pieces, like *Nests of Cups*, composed of four or six small vases, the handles of which are entwined together; a sort of perforated stand for boiled eggs, *tea-pots* and *caddies;* the money-boxes of three tiers, on the top of which is represented the allegory of the hen and chickens, we shall have exhausted the list of the shapes upon which the old English Slip Potter displays his ingenuity.

We shall now return to those productions so characteristic of the art of the old English Potter, the *Tygs*, which well deserve a special notice and a few words of description. An indefinite number of handles applied to a large cup of coarse clay distinguishes, as we have just said, the *Tyg* from other vessels of early times. Drinking cups furnished in that manner were manufactured at Wrotham, and in several other places in England, but the term *Tyg* does not seem to have been used out of the Staffordshire Potteries district. It is probably a corruption in the local dialect from the Roman word *Tegula*, a "tile;" a word which in Italian has become *Tegola*, in Spanish *Teja*, in old German *Tieghel*, in French *Tuile*, etc. Bosworth, in his "Anglo-Saxon Dictionary," gives the name *Tigel*, "a tile, a brick, anything made of clay, a pot, a vessel." Posset and other compound drinks were brewed in the *Tyg* at social gatherings. It stood in the middle of the table, and each guest helped himself to its contents; in its use it was not unlike the Greek *crater*, a capacious vase containing a mixed beverage, out of which a slave filled the cups all round; but as slaves did not wait at old English convivial meetings, the common cup was provided on every side with convenient handles, in order that each guest could draw it to himself. Cups or glasses were dispensed with, every one drinking from the

FIG. 17. VARIOUS SHAPES OF TYGS.

pot. A curious passage in *William of Malmesbury* says, "Formerly the vessels were regularly divided for to prevent quarrels. King Edward commanded the drinking vessels to be made with knobs in the inside at certain distance from each other, and decreted that no person, under a certain penalty, should either himself drink or compel another to drink at one draught more than from one of these knobs to the other."

The earliest Tygs were provided with only two handles placed closely together, so that two friends sitting on the same bench had each one side to drink from. The shapes were first of all straight and narrow, and the decoration consisted of applied pieces of light-coloured clay,

Fig. 18. Tyg.—Mr. H. Willett's Coll.

stamped in separate moulds; subsequently they became shorter and more open at the mouth, and slip, poured on the surface in fine traceries, was alone used (Fig. 17).

The number of handles was sometimes eight, and each was double or triple in its height (Fig. 18); the shape sometimes concealed a curious contrivance like a whistle or a puzzle.

All the applied parts were made by hand with twisted and crumpled bits of clay, much in the same fashion as those to be seen on the old British glass found in the barrows; there is the same disposition and the same treatment. A Tyg bears a striking likeness to an Anglo-Saxon drinking cup.

We have given in our first edition a Tyg inscribed "*Mary Shifilbottom*, 1705." It is one of the last period; the four rudimental handles have no longer the same importance as in the early specimens. The potter who spelt in this way the old name of Shufflebottom was certainly not a scholar, but considering the state of education at that time, we may be astonished that the posset pot maker of Staffordshire could even write at all. We may notice that most of the inscribed drinking cups were presented to ladies. We should on that account say that these Tygs were more an object of adornment for the shelves of the housewife than for utility, and were only taken down on very special occasions. That is perhaps why so many have been preserved to us, which otherwise would have disappeared like pieces in common use, now become so scarce; handed down from father to son as a sort of heirloom, they have thus escaped destruction.

Tygs disappeared completely when the use of earthenware became more general, and mugs or other vessels were manufactured in bulk for the table. The intercourse, created by the increase of trade, between the people of Staffordshire and those of the neighbouring counties, drove the local custom away. Loving cups, that is, large cups having one handle on each side, were still made in tortoiseshell or salt-glaze ware, and upon them the workman displayed his greatest skill; but as early as the beginning of the 18th century he abandoned the numberless combinations of handles which he had been so proud of setting round his favourite pieces. The custom of every guest drinking an honoured toast out of the same cup did not pass away altogether, but the vessel was no longer made in a style recalling that especial purpose. A posset pot in our collection bears the inscription, "*The best is not too good,*" written round the top in the usual black slip letters, studded over with yellow dots, and underneath are two initials, "H. L.," with the date "1714." We are in doubt as to the true meaning of the motto. Was it that, even at that date, the delicate and refined *Elers* ware was still so little known that this Posset Pot, with its rough decoration of slip, was considered as one of the best possible works in clay? We prefer supposing that it only alluded to the quality of the mixtures brewed in it.

As through their works the names of the

greater men in art have come down to posterity, so the few works of the old Staffordshire Potters which have escaped destruction have saved from oblivion the names of several of those modest artists. Why should we not call them artists? In our own estimation they well deserve that name, if we consider how unpropitious to their development was the low condition in which they moved. Some excuse may be found for the roughness of their drawing in the fact that the taste for fine art was only just beginning to dawn upon England, and good examples were altogether unknown to them; it is to their credit that, labouring under such adverse circumstances, they energetically endeavoured to raise themselves above the common level. We must also take into account, not only their insufficient education, but also the simple wants their industry was called upon to supply. Staffordshire was then far from being a wealthy county; what need was there for a more refined ware? The agriculturists and small tradesmen who sparsely populated the district would not readily have chosen goods made more expensive by mere workmanship. They were satisfied with the common crocks, and the craving for the possession of any articles of luxury was not yet born in so primitive a community. The few specimens upon which the potter tried to outdo his ordinary work were those he perfected for the gratification of his own pride, or as presents to some friend or patron, to whom he desired to offer an uncommon sample of his skill, but he did not consider them as articles of his current trade. Those belonging to that exceptional class all bear witness to that feeling; they are inscribed, "*The best is not too good for you.*" "*This cup I made for you and so no more,*" etc.

FIG 19. OWL JUG, MARBLED WARE—MR. H. WILLETT'S COLL.

As to the common ware, it was decorated with marbling. While the ground was still in the wet state, lines of brown slip were poured upon the yellow clay, and then with a many-pointed tool, made of wire or leather, like those used by the wood grainer, they were combed down to imitate the veining of marble, and so an unlimited variety of effects was easily obtainable (Fig 19). An excavation seldom takes place at Hanley or Burslem without bringing to the surface heaps of fragments of this ware, but complete pieces are getting very scarce, and are, indeed, almost unobtainable; nearly all specimens now preserved by collectors have been dug out of the ground where they had been thrown away as imperfect by the maker. Half a century ago ware of this kind was still commonly used by poor people, but it has now completely disappeared.

In the list of names preserved to us, that of *Thomas Toft* stands first. He was of an old Catholic family, which has still many branches in the Potteries. One of his descendants worked for *Josiah Wedgwood* towards the close of the last century, and had his medallion made at the works at an advanced age. The name of Toft is still common in Holland, and M. Thooft is now the head of one of the present manufactories of Delft; perhaps a distant connection could be traced between the Dutch and the Staffordshire potter. From about 1660, *Thomas Toft* added to the manufacture of usual ware the making of those huge platters, the rims of which are ornamented with a trellis-work of orange and brown slip, and the centre adorned with a conventional flower, a curious figure, a lion, or an eagle. No doubt he never thought of deriving his inspiration from nature, but rather from such bits of heraldry, coins, or common effigies of Royal personages as might have come under his notice. He is generally spoken of as a potter of Burslem, but we know that he worked in a lane between Shelton and Newcastle-under-Lyme; one of his dishes has been seen at a cottage at Hanley, bearing, besides his name written in slip on the face, this inscription scratched in at the back, "*Thomas Toft, Tinker's Clough.—I made it—166. .*" The place still bears the same name in our day. He was probably the first to attempt such an ambitious style as the representation of human figures; many admirers and plagiarists emulated him almost immediately. Whatever the maker's name may have been, most of these dishes seem to have been reproductions, or at least imitations, of one master.

Simeon Shaw *(Chemistry of Pottery)* attributes to *Thomas Toft* the introduction of an "aluminous shale or fire-brick clay," a somewhat obscure statement; but the enumeration Shaw gives of the different improvements by *Toft's* contemporaries shows that the worthy historian of the Staffordshire Potteries is not always to be relied upon. His information was negligently gathered, and appears to be based mainly on unreliable hearsay. In many cases we know for certain that he has been misinformed, and we are warranted therefore in suspecting that most of his assertions stand in need of corroboration. Without attempting to give a complete list of all the dishes signed by Thomas Toft, preserved in the National Museum and private collections, we may, however, enumerate the following pieces, all adorned on the rim with the usual trellis-work, and inscribed with the name in full.

Museum of Practical Geology—A Crowned Lion.
South Kensington Museum—A Mermaid.
„ „ „ —The Lion and Unicorn.
Bateman Museum.—Half length figure of Charles II.
Collection, T. Hulmes—Conventional Flower.
„ *H. T. Davenport*—Duke of York.
„ „ —Double-headed Eagle.
„ *A. H. Church*—A Pelican.
„ *L. Solon*—A Cavalier Drinking a Toast.

To this list can be added a few other dishes which have passed into various hands and which we have lost sight of. He seldom signed any cups or tygs; yet a four-handled pot, bearing his name, is preserved in the York Museum.

The subjects represented were generally such as appealed to the imagination. Sometimes the decoration consisted of marvellous and hyperbolical flowers or monstrous animals, though more frequently preference was given to the figures of the King and his Queen, personages who in the minds of the simple inhabitants of the outlandish districts were looked upon as almost supernatural. In the same manner as the Italian artist exerted his fancy in designing the mythological gods, the angels, or the saints, the potter of Staffordshire tried to represent royalty, of which he formed a conception quite as confused and conventional. It would certainly be difficult to be less realistic than *Thomas Toft* has been in the treatment of his royal groups.

The name of *Ralph Toft* occurs on several dishes of similar make. One of them, dated 1677, has a figure of a soldier holding a sword in each hand, with a crowned head on a medallion right and left of the principal subject. We find this crowned head very often repeated; we have it on a large dish, where in an arrangement with four fleurs-de-lys, it forms an ornamental rosette; again it appears on another specimen in our own collection on each side of the half-length figure of a queen, inscribed *Ralph oft*, the *T* having evidently been omitted by mistake. In the Salford Museum a *Ralph Toft* dish has, with the name, the date 1676.

John Wright, 1707, from a dish in the Wedgwood Institute, Burslem. *W. Rich, 1702*, (Shaw). *T. Johnson, 1694*, in the collection of the late Rev. W. Sibthorpe.

William Sans is mentioned by Chaffers as having also made dishes of similar character.

William Taylor, from a dish in the Bateman Museum, with two full-length figures in the costume of the time of the Stuarts, and from another in our own possession.

George Taylor, with also two full-length figures.

Joseph Glass, of Hanley, whose manufactory was in existence in 1710, and who must have produced a very fine ware of the sort, if we may judge from the beautiful fragments dug up at the place

FIG. 20. POSSET POT.

only a few years ago. One of his works is in the collection of the Rev. T. Staniforth (Fig. 20); it is a four-handled tyg, bearing *Glass's* name, and the usual slip designs in brown on a buff ground. Mr. H. Griffiths, of Brighton, has a cradle inscribed *Joseph Glass*, and we should also ascribe to him a remarkably large cradle, of the same style, inscribed William Smith on one side and Martha Smith on the other; at the end a crowned effigy surmounts the date, 1700 (Fig. 21).

By the number still to be found in Staffordshire, where these cradles were made, either of Slip-decorated ware, Salt-glaze, or Cream-colour, we may infer that presents of this sort were a tradition peculiar to the district.

FIG. 21. SLIP-DECORATED CRADLE. COLL. L. S.

Pottery is not only associated with the material necessities of man, but also with his feelings and affections, and has from the most ancient times been used to commemorate some momentous event in his career. An early British urn speaks to us of death and mysterious burial rites; a cradle of brown clay recalls the christening festivities in families of the Midland counties in the seventeenth century. The potter has always taken a pleasure in putting his best work upon presents intended for his friends. In France, on the morning that followed the wedding, an *écuelle*, or nicely decorated covered bowl with two handles, was always offered by the guests to the married couple. In England, on the occasion of the birth of a first child, a cradle made of clay or precious material was presented to the parents; the custom has not died out altogether, for on a similar occurrence such a testimonial is presented by subscription to a man holding a public office. These earthenware cradles were worked up in the plainest fashion; no moulds or models were required, and any workman could make them. Some flattened bats joined together sufficed for the shape, and knobs, rolled in the hands, were stuck on every corner by way of decoration. Some of them were afterwards ornamented with an inscription or a pattern of coloured slip.

Another cradle in our possession has the name of *Ralph Simpson*, and the same name occurs upon a slip dish, with the figures of William and Mary. Not fewer than three *Simpsons* figure in the list of potters established at Burslem in 1710. On this list, drawn up by *Josiah Wedgwood*, and given by Miss Meteyard, many other potters of the time are recorded, but it would be very difficult to identify their respective productions.

With a few exceptions, seldom do we find any name on a piece, and if we do find one it generally refers to the person to whom it was dedicated, especially in the cases of tygs, cradles, jugs, etc.

We feel inclined to suppose that if *Thomas Toft* repeated so many times his bold signature on his remarkable dishes, he did it with the view of presenting them to his best customers and patrons, not only as grateful testimonials for past favours, but also as an advertisement likely to bring further orders by the admiration they could not fail to excite. Thus, kept in some country dealer's window as the most conspicuous object in the display, or perhaps set on the dresser of the best room of the house, they remained for long years, becoming heirlooms in the family, until one day, neglected by their possessors, they fell into the hands of the collector.

The huge platters *Thomas Toft* has signed are so numerous that the generic name of Toft dishes has been accepted for all the Slip-decorated ones made in his time. We shall describe in a few words one of the dishes which may be considered as being of the best manner. With some slight variation, this description may be applied to all the others. The body of the dish is of coarse marl, washed on the inside with a coat of fine yellow clay: it is highly fired, very heavy and resistant. The outline of the subject is traced with brown slip punctuated with white dots; the interspaces are filled in with orange colour; in the middle stand a quaint figure, or a curious animal; three flowers, a distant reminiscence of fleurs-de-lys, and a sort of uncouth garland completes the subject; on the broad rim, brown and orange slips have been trailed to form a close trellis-work. The whole is very effective, and if we consider the decoration only as a means of bringing out the contrast of colours, we may pass over the oddity of its execution. We have heard critics dismiss such pieces in a few words, to the effect that they are no better than the barbarous works of New Zealanders; but why this should not be taken as a compliment instead of condemnation we fail to perceive. We do not in any way despise the carvings of the clubs and canoe heads of the savage; they exhibit a real understanding of what can make them rich and beautiful, display a fanciful combination of lines and proportions that owes nothing to servile imitation, and strikingly shows what are the earliest and most natural notions of decoration that can bud out from the untutored fancy of a human being. The archaic creations of the early Etruscans and Greeks contain in their roughness all the germs of what was one day to be the art of Praxiteles and Phidias, and this none the less for their being in some respects akin to the works of some Polynesian savages. Shall we pass an irrevocable sentence upon the old Slip Potter on account of his imperfections? At least his trials forcibly tell us about obsolete tastes and forgotten customs; they make us acquainted with the state of artistic education in his times, pottery in all ages reflecting the condition of every other branch of art; we see how meritorious these old workmen were in following up unremittingly emendations and improvements, and how a genuine and even refined style was to be the result of their primitive and uncouth labours.

To the slip dish made to pattern succeeded another sort of production exhibiting a greater freedom in the imagination of the primitive artist. In some cases his humoristic turn of mind would burst out into some rough caricature, somewhat childish in execution. You are welcome to laugh at the grotesque performance of the jolly and funny old potter; the dish was never intended for aught but to induce a gentle merriment. Do not forget that the maker never anticipated that he was working for you or me, the sensitive and squeamish children of a refined century, and that he might one day have to undergo our criticism. The noble and solemn

Greek interred his vases in stately tombs, foreseeing that in after ages they would come out, proclaiming the elevation of his thoughts and the splendour of his art. The rough workman of Staffordshire did his work on the spur of the moment; it was a morning's joke, destined to be forgotten by the evening.

We have already seen how few were the means, patterns, and processes, at the disposal of the Slip Potter when he wanted to complete a piece that would surpass all his daily productions. The broad and quaint slip letters, acquiring a peculiar shape of their own by the way in which they were poured on, often came in as the main feature of decoration, and we know of many examples where they make a graceful ornament merely by the variety of their lines. Sometimes they were accompanied by huge Elizabethan flowers, very conventional in their shape, and seldom varied in their arrangement; whether brown upon yellow, or light upon the dark colour, they contrast boldly with the ground, and frequently the same piece offers both combinations.

Besides the decoration with slip poured on the surface, another process often resorted to is the blending together of red and yellow slip, in imitation of marble; it is seen on the owl-jugs, and on some curious puzzle jugs; in fewer instances, the upper coat of light clay was scratched so as to show the dark ground, in the same manner as the Italian *Sgrafiato* (Fig. 22).

Additional portions modelled by hand were sometimes applied. In the Hanley Museum is

FIG. 22. SGRAFIATO JUG—NOTTINGHAM MUSEUM.

a jug (Fig. 23), dated 1693, which has a figure of Plenty modelled in front; some thin strips of clay were also laid on and deeply notched with a tool; they have a brilliant effect under the glaze, and constitute another means of decoration also frequently used.

Jugs decorated with slip are seldom met with; not that they were rarely made, but probably because, being of a more handy shape than a tyg or an ornamental dish, they shared the fate of all common crockery in use, and were soon destroyed. Not much value seems ever to have been put upon such jugs, or mugs of the same description; they are never found mounted with silver or pewter, like those made

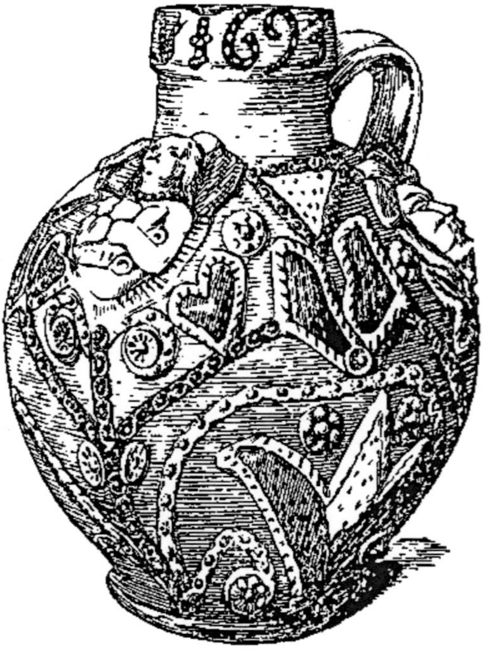

FIG. 23. SLIP-DECORATED JUG—HANLEY MUSEUM.

of Stone-ware in the South of England, nor do we ever see them mentioned in any will or other documents. However carefully finished might have been a special piece of this sort, it was always considered as one of the common productions of the place.

In no case do we see any moulded parts side by side with the works of the oldest Slip potters of Staffordshire, as we observe on the slip pieces of southern origin. They borrowed little indeed from the rest of the world; the absence of oxide of copper upon their early pieces, when we know that in other countries that material had been used for centuries, would tend to prove that these worthies confined themselves to their own discoveries. The pigments were very limited, being confined to the white, yellow, red, and orange slips. If we occasionally notice a grey slip on the buff ground, it is due to the discolouration of the orange, through an excess of smoke in the oven.

The traditional manner of employing the slips never varied, and could not lead to many improvements. The flowers and letters were freely poured on the surface, without any tracing to guide the hand; and the lines thus produced resulted in a design which could never show much delicacy or elaboration of treatment; yet when stamping and casting began to be introduced, the slip-decorator found out a way of availing himself of some of the new-fangled methods employed by the more spirited potters working contemporaneously with him. Then we begin to see dishes, the intended decoration of which had been incised and carved on the block upon which they were pressed; thus all the outlines stood out in relief on the bat of clay which was formed into a platter, and a space was reserved between the two ridges, leaving a hollow to be filled in by slips of divers colours. On these examples the off-hand execution has given place to a process which provides against any mistake being made in the pouring out of the colour through a quill. Upon such a form many pieces of the same pattern could be pressed, and the work of the decorator consisted merely in filling in with the two coloured slips the cavities prepared to receive them, a process which, by the bye, has some analogy to the "cloisonné" enamelling on copper. The designs so treated are much more complicated than those seen on the usual Slip dishes. In the first edition of this work we have etched two dishes decorated by this process. One of them has again royalty for its subject. A portrait of a king, George I. or George II., occupies the centre, and is surrounded with a deer and two birds, emblematic of hunting being one of the royal prerogatives. The head is no longer traced with the conventional scrolls which stand for the features of *T. Toft's* kings, but is evidently copied from some good portrait or engraving. This is certainly a step in advance, but the picture adds little to the real merit of the work, which consists in the richness of the glaze and the deep tone of the various slips. The other may be one of the sarcastic presents customarily sent on St. Valentine's day. A neighbour's wife, or perhaps his own, had shown herself somewhat liable to the white sin of curiosity or interference, and to her the anonymous potter sends this cutting allegory. In the dish are depicted Lot's wife, two angels blowing trumpets, and the pillar of salt; and for fear that the intention should not be forcibly enough expressed, an inscription is added, "*Remember Lot's Wife*," with the date, "1727," to show that it was intended to relate to some particular occurrence. Scriptural jokes were freely indulged in between the period succeeding the Reformation and the appearance of Methodism, which altered so much the manners of the people in the Potteries district.

In Mr. Willett's collection is a very remarkable one, illustrating the popular saying, "*A bird in the hand is worth two in the bush.*" Notches are, as a rule, to be noticed on the edges of these dishes; they answered a double purpose, they were ornamental, and prevented the dish, which was fired downwards, from sticking to the bats upon which it rested. In any case the glazing remains the same; it is the rich and lustrous *Galena* unsparingly dusted on, which, liquefied by the firing, spreads upon the piece, if we may say so, like golden treacle. In

France the same material was used under the name of *Alquifou*. Though its high colouration forbids its use to any depth on any light ware, it becomes unrivalled when it is intended to varnish a clay already of a dark colour. Few things, indeed, can hold their own by the side of a mellow-toned and richly-glazed slip piece. We remember once coming across an old Staffordshire dish exhibited in a dealer's window, amidst a host of very handsome "curios," porcelain of all sorts, Oriental silks, and chased silver and gold. The eye that had rested upon the uncouth platter could hardly leave it, and was attracted to it over and over again, so powerful and harmonious did it look amongst all the other treasures. Need we say that we secured it, and were more proud of its possession than if we had been permitted to carry away the most costly of the objects by which it was surrounded?

It is said that in Persia the productions of the most ancient potteries, even though mere fragments, are bought by their admirers at high prices, to be mounted in precious metals with all the skill that the modern workman can command. The same idea was carried out in France in the last century to enhance the beauty of antique Chinese pieces. The coarsest specimens of "Celadon" or "Rouge Flambé" have been set by "*Gouttieres*" and other celebrated chasers in bronzes of the most refined workmanship. In England also this tribute of admiration has been paid by a few collectors of great taste to some of the rough fictile gems of the past. Not to speak of the time when the first stone-ware pots used to be elaborately mounted by the silversmith, we know of some instances where a similar sort of setting has been successfully attempted; we regret to say that the examples are only too few. The contrast obtained between some roughly-made and deeply-coloured earthen utensils, mellowed by age, and the sharply detailed and glittering metal-work produces an amazing effect.

We have said that inscriptions are one of the main features of old Staffordshire decoration; they are not only interesting in that respect, but also are worthy of notice by the humour and sometimes even the pathos which they evince. It is a notorious fact that writing is a prominent constituent of decoration with nations among whom learning has not yet been widely spread. From the Egyptian priests who committed the everlasting evidence of their knowledge to the walls of palaces and temples in symbolic figurations which adepts alone could decipher, to the Moors of Spain, who brought writing into play amongst their intricate arabesques, so as to make of it the more graceful part of the whole tracery, every nation has considered inscriptions, when introduced in their early artistic productions, architectural or ceramic, as answering a twofold purpose, that is to say, not only to be commemorative of some important event, or memorable date, but also to add more beauty to the general ornamentation. But as the level of education rises in the masses, in the same proportion the letter loses its ornamental character, and its use becomes neglected and obsolete; in fact one might say that inscriptions cease to be employed as a means of decoration at the precise time when everyone is able to understand them. It will, we hope, interest the reader if we give here a few of the inscriptions we have gathered from old pieces of Staffordshire ware.

In our own collection :—

"THE BEST IS NOT TOO GOOD, 1714,"

in brown slip upon a two-handled and covered posset pot.

"THE GIFT IS SMALL
BUT LOVE IS ALL, 1725,"

scratched in clay upon a brown glazed cradle.

"REMEMBER LOT'S WIFE, 1727,"

upon a yellow dish decorated with brown and red slip.

Several names on tygs, probably those of the persons to whom they were given:

"MARGRETE COLLEY, 1684."
"JOHN HUGHES, 1690."
"MARY SHIFFILBOTTOM, 1705."

In the Museum of the Somerset Archæological Society :—

"THREE MERRY BOYS, 1697,"

on a nest of cups; the entwined handles are pierced, and allow the liquor to run from one cup to the other.

In the Norwich Museum :—

"COME BROTHER SHALL WE JOIN,
GIVE ME YOUR TWO PENCE HERE IS MINE.
WAYMAN, 1670,"

on a brown jug decorated with slip.

Mentioned by Mr. W. Bemrose in "The Pottery and Porcelain of Derbyshire,"

"GOD BLES THE QUEEN AND PRENCE GORGE
DRINK BE MERY & MARY B B
JOHN MIER MADE THIS CUP 1708."

In Mr. Geo. T. Robinson's collection :—

"ROBART POOL MAD THIS CUP
WITH A GUD POSSET FIL AND (DRINK IT UP,)"

on a three-handled posset pot.

In the Liverpool Museum :—

"BREAK ME NOT I PRAY IN YOUER HAST
FOR I TO NONE WILL GIVE DESTAST 1651."

In the Salisbury Museum :—

"HERE IS THE GEST OF BARLY KORNE
GLAD HAM I THE CILD IS BORN
I G 1692."

In the possession of Sir Ivor B. Guest (see Chaffers' Marks and Monograms):—

"COME GOOD WOMAN DRINK OF THE BEST
YOU MY LADY AND ALL THE REST,"

upon a brown four-handled tyg.

In Mr. H. Willett's collection, Brighton:—

"ANN DRAPER THIS CUP I MADE FOR YOU & SO NO MORE.—J. W., 1707,"

upon a brown and yellow posset pot.

"THE RIT GENURAL CORNAL FOR THE DROWNKEN REGIMENT,"

on a large beer jug.

The alphabet in square compartments and the date, "*May the 29 Day, 1706*," on a large posset pot.

In the British Museum:—

"REMEMBER THY END TRULY,"

upon a pot of questionable shape.

Specimens of what we might call "speaking pottery" are somewhat limited in number, as the style is confined to presentation pieces, reverentially preserved in old families. They were so difficult to obtain that we do not find any in the collection of Enoch Wood, who had shown himself so zealous in collecting all that could be interesting for the history of the old Staffordshire ware, and yet had probably been unable to secure any.

During the latter part of the last century the

art of slip was superseded by more advanced processes of decoration; however, in the Liverpool Museum is a brown puzzle jug bearing a long inscription, very neatly poured on, on which we read the date 1828. At the present day, in the market places of Norfolk, Kent, and Lancashire, are daily sold coarse pots and pancheons which are streaked here and there with lines and scrolls of white slip, made in some remote country pot works. In Switzerland the tradition is still kept up, though it has lost many of its ancient characteristics, and the peasant's ware continues to be made pleasant and gaudy by the use of different coloured clays poured on the ground in the same manner as of old.

In Italy, also, a ware of the same sort is extensively fabricated, and it requires a very skilful hand to dash on at one stroke, with the liquid slip, the conventional flowers and animals that suit the taste of the people. A Milan manufacturer having engaged for that special work a pastry cook, who was extremely clever at embellishing his cakes with designs in syrups and currants, has found his talents so successful when thus directed to pot painting, and his work meet with such a demand, that he realises more profit out of the extemporised artist than he would out of half-a-dozen china painters.

May we be excused if we show ourselves a

little partial to the slip process, considering that it is closely connected with "*Pâte sur Pâte,*" a process that we have practised ourselves for more than twenty-five years, and which is also painting in slip upon the unbaked surface?

We shall conclude by mentioning another sort of slip-ware also made now-a-days, the sham "old slip," of which we have to confess the possession of several pieces, bought at a high figure for genuine specimens. We wish our experience to be of some use to other collectors, and hope our readers may be spared the disappointment of finding that a piece bought in a lonely cottage from a respectable-looking old woman, turns out to be nothing but an impudent forgery! "Forewarned, forearmed."

CHAPTER IV.

ENGLISH DELFT.

Dutch-ware.—Its Body and Glaze.—Delft made in England—Lambeth—Liverpool—Bristol—The Staffordshire Potteries.—English Delft Dishes.—Unsuccessful Attempts to Manufacture Delft in the Potteries.—Inscriptions.—English Delft only made as an Imitation of Foreign Ware.

FIG. 24. ENGLISH DELFT DISH. WILLIAM AND MARY—COLL. L. S.

ENGLISH DELFT.

FROM Holland, where an ever-increasing number of factories of the white ware coated with stanniferous enamel had already reached the highest degree of artistic and commercial development, the process was brought into England about the middle of the seventeenth century. It was the nearest approach to the Oriental porcelain, which was so much admired, and so difficult to obtain. The Dutch, who imported those rarities from the West Indies, endeavoured to transform into a plausible substitute the common white faïence they were then making, and by decorating it in blue with subjects copied from Chinese pieces, to realise, if not the unobtainable transparence, at least all the outward looks of the Eastern China. They succeeded in producing such a close imitation that some of the blue and white Delft dishes might, at a distance, deceive the eye of even a connoisseur.

The body is of a yellowish or red colour, very friable and porous; carbonate of lime enters largely into its composition. The glaze, a thick and opaque enamel, is a mixture of oxides of lead and tin. Its manufacture differed from all other early ware in this respect, that it had to be fired twice; once, to harden the biscuit, so as to allow of its being dipped in the liquid glaze, the porosity of the body absorbing the water while the enamel remained on the surface; and then a second time, to vitrify the glaze.

The earliest dated pieces considered to be English Delft, that is to say potted in England, were probably made with clay from Holland, as we may infer from the fact of their substance being very porous, and easy to cut into with a knife, from its effervescing with nitric acid, and at a high temperature melting into a coarse glass. The native clays, however, were soon brought into use, and then we find the ware has been highly fired, and can hardly be scratched with a sharp point. It is of some importance to remark that the list of all the British clays drawn up by Mr. Maw, and published in the catalogue of the Jermyn Street Museum, does not contain any calcareous clay like that which constitutes the principal element of the foreign stanniferous faïence. However, the ware was made in England with the local materials, only the biscuit being dense instead of spongy does not when dipped retain a sufficiently thick coating of enamel, and its red colour shows through, giving the ware that rosy tint so often observed by collectors; crazing is generally seen on the surface, through want of affinity between body and glaze. Dutch pieces, on the contrary, are as a rule free from this defect. The English potter was so well aware of this shortcoming that the early dishes were coated only on the front side, the back being glazed with the usual lead glaze, and sometimes mottled with ordinary tortoiseshell colours. Whenever the style of painting, which otherwise is the safest guide for identification, appears doubtful, this should be sufficient to indicate the origin of a piece. Dutch dishes may be found similar in design, but they are invariably enamelled on both sides; as to the few dishes of Italian make which possess the same peculiarity of being glazed with lead on the back, their decoration is so characteristic that in their case a mistake is almost impossible.

England was not long in following upon the track of the Dutch potters who manufactured in the town of Delft the first pieces of stanniferous faïence, decorated with blue and other colours. M. H. Havard in his remarkable book has established in a peremptory manner, that no potworks where such ware was made, existed in the town before the beginning of the seventeenth century, contrary to the belief generally accredited, and it is only at the date of 1600 that he found such manufactories mentioned for the first time in the official records. It is for us a fact worthy of remark that the oldest authenticated specimen of blue painted ware made at Delft is signed by an Englishman, one *Tome Jansz*, a Dutch mis-spelling, which conceals but imperfectly the British name of Tom Jones; a soldier, who is described as having been "born in England, beyond London," and who came to Holland with the English regiment commanded by Captain Hamwout (?) This interesting work is a dish painted with the Last Judgment, a subject comprising four hundred figures of the painter's own composition, and made by him in the factory of Herman Pietersz towards 1600.

The white and painted earthenware must have been made in or near London, about the year 1668, as appears from the record of a lawsuit instituted by one *Edmund Warner* against the Custom House authorities, who had seized one of the parcels of potters' clay which he used to import from Holland. The trial took place in 1693, and five London potters gave evidence as to the clay being of the kind they had constantly bought from the said Warner for above 25 years. (Catalogue of the Museum of Practical Geology, p. 300. Appendix.)

At the date of 1676 a patent was taken out by *John Arien Von Hamme*, for the sole practise of "the art of making tiles, porcelain, and other earthenware, after the way practised in Holland, which has not been practised in this our kingdom." On the register of the St. Lucas' Guild, preserved at Delft, mention is made of one Jan Ariensz Van Hammen, who was received master *plateel-backer* in 1661, and who is evidently the same to whom this patent was granted. It would be difficult to reconcile J. A. Van Hamme's pretension of having introduced the trade into England, with the fact that many pieces bearing an unmistakably English stamp are found inscribed with a much earlier date than that of his patent. Thus a Delft-ware mug in the Jermyn Street Museum is dated 1631, and inscribed "*William & Elizabeth Burges;*" another in Mr. Willett's possession is painted with the name of "*John Leman*, 1634." One may assume that towards the same period English-made tiles were extensively in use for interior decoration. Bottles of Delft-ware were commonly used to keep foreign wines in; they were all dated in blue pencilling to record the year in which the wine had been bottled (Fig. 25). We find them with "Sack, 1649," "Claret, 1648," "Whit, 1648," etc. One of a larger size, in the Norwich Museum has the Grocers' Arms, the monogram E $\overset{W}{M}$ E, and the date, 1649. None have been found to be dated later than 1659.

Sets of three or four cups, with their handles entwined (an essentially English shape), were made in Delft as well as in Slip-ware. A mug in the South Kensington Museum is inscribed, "*Ann Chapman*, 1649." Many pieces bear the

FIG. 25. SACK BOTTLE.—COLL. L. S.

arms of the City Companies. Mr. A. Franks has one with the arms of the Bakers' Company, 1657, and another with the Leathersellers', 1660. In the Bohn collection was a quaint-shaped cup, with the portrait of Charles II., and the motto, "*Be merry and wise*, 1660." A cup in Professor Church's collection had "*God save the King*, 1662," inscribed under a crown. We possess a cup, with twisted handle, with the monogram $\overset{R}{A\ I}$ disposed in the English manner, the top letter standing for the surname, and the other two for the Christian name of the husband and wife, and the date, 1667.

Two very important documents referring to the making of Delft-ware in England are given by R. W. Binns in the appendix of his work—"A Century of Potting in the City of Worcester." (Second edition.) The first is a petition addressed to the king, Charles II., November, 1676, by several potters of the City of London: namely, John Ariens Van Haunne (the same again who appears in the specifications of patents at the date of October, 1676, as J. A. Van Hamme), James Barston, Daniel Parker, John Campion, Richard Newman, and divers others who complain that "notwithstanding the statute of Edward IV. prohibiting the bringing in of any painted wares into this kingdom by way of merchandise," etc., "several persons have presumed to import and daily to bring in several great quantities of painted earthenwares," etc., "to the inevitable ruin of the petitioners, and many hundreds of poor men, women, and children, whose subsistence and livelihood depend thereon, and the total destruction of the manufacture here, which is fully as well done as any foreign, and with most materials of English growth," etc.

There is not the slightest doubt here about

which sort of ware is intended. Painted ware at that time could be no other than Delft or stanniferous faïence, such as was introduced in England by the Dutchman, T. A. Van Hamme. The second document is still more explicit. It is a proclamation of Charles II., dated 1672, from which we shall quote the following:—"Whereas the art of making all sorts of painted earthenwares is a mystery, but lately found out in England," etc., "notwithstanding which divers merchants and others have lately imported into England great quantities of the like painted earthenwares, from parts beyond the seas, and do sell the same at an under value to the great discouragement of so useful a manufacture lately found out," etc. "We therefore," etc., "charge and command that from henceforth no person, native or foreigner, do or shall import, bring, send, or convey" "from or out of any place or part beyond the seas," "any kind or sort of painted earthenware whatsoever (except those of china, and stone bottles and jugs), by way of merchandise," etc., "that no person that now uses the trade of retailing, selling, or uttering of any painted earthenware (except those of china, and stone bottles, and jugs), shall at any time hereafter buy, bargain, or contract for or concerning the importation of any painted earthenware, made beyond the sea or in any other place out of our said realm of England," etc., "upon pain of being grievously fined," etc

We can elicit from the above that, not only had the industry of the potter already been thought of sufficient importance to be protected against foreign competition, even prior to this petition being addressed to the king by the potters of London (considering that the royal proclamation is four years earlier in date), but we are also led to surmise by the tenor of these documents that the manufacture of Delft-ware must have preceded, or have been deemed more worthy of attention than that of stone-ware, since the protection is not extended to "stone bottles and jugs."

Drug pots, inscribed in English with the name of their contents, and pill-slabs, are generally ascribed to Lambeth. The production of English Delft became very important in that locality, for it is said that at one time twenty factories were occupied in making it. Though it never became general in England, the manufacture was established in some of the seaports which had a regular trade with Holland. At Liverpool it was for a time the "principal trade of the town," according to the Holt & Gregson MSS., quoted by Mr. Charles T. Gatty, from whom we borrow the following extracts:—"To stone building (1660) there succeeded brick and slate building in Liverpool. To brickmaking succeeded the clay potteries. To them Delft-ware. To the Delft-ware succeeded the whole flint or Queen-ware in 1760, by *Wedgwood.* The Delft-ware, every merchant of note in Liverpool was concerned in early in the 18th century." The progression in the different branches of the trade is plainly described, yet, in this case also, pieces authenticated by tradition carry us back to a still earlier period. A Delft mug in the Liverpool Museum, attributed to Liverpool manufacture, is inscribed, "*John Williamson,* 1645." If we can implicitly trust its evidence, the ware had been manufactured long before the period referred to by the writer.

In 1716 the English Delft had already been brought near to perfection, as we can see by the large plaque preserved in the Mayer Museum; it is painted in blue, with a view of Great Crosby, the landscape being plentifully diversified with ships, houses, figures, and animals of all sorts. In the old church at Crosby may also be seen a plaque of the same ware, with the arms of the Merchant Taylors' Company, and the date, 1722. At that time the ware was already exported in large quantities, and numberless examples have been preserved to us dating far down in the eighteenth century. Among these may be mentioned tiles for fire-places, with blue landscapes and figure subjects; puzzle jugs of elegant shape (Fig. 26), thinly potted and brightly glazed, with doggrel verses painted all round; and especially large punch bowls, decorated with a ship in full sail, and a border of Chinese flowers. On these the blue painting is so cleverly executed that they vie with many a piece made in Holland, and the artists had nothing more to learn from their masters. *Shaw* and *Pennington* were very celebrated for their punch bowls between 1750 and 1780. The Mayer Museum

FIG. 26. DELFT PUZZLE JUG.—COLL. L. S.

has one $17\frac{1}{2}$ inches in diameter. Another of the same style in the Jermyn Street Museum is $20\frac{1}{2}$ inches in diameter. In the Mechanics' Institution at Hanley, another bowl, also $20\frac{1}{2}$ inches in diameter, is rendered particularly interesting by the label accompanying it, which has been written by the painter himself: "*John Robinson, a pot painter, served his time at Pennington's, in*

Shaw's Brow, and there painted this punch bowl." They are all of them masterpieces of the craft.

At Vauxhall and Mortlake, Delft-ware potteries were carried on, but no specimens have been so far identified as coming from these places.

At Bristol, English Delft was extensively manufactured from the beginning of the eighteenth century, but the potters of that city never attained to the degree of perfection which the art reached at Liverpool. The glaze is far from being so bright, some of the colours are dull, and lack the gloss usually noticed on the fine stanniferous enamel. A plate painted in blue, dated 1703, and a high-heeled shoe, dated 1727, are referred to Bristol manufacture. Tiles for house decoration were painted, so as to form, when put together, a large panel. Thus the Jermyn Street Museum has a set made at *Richard Franks'*, 1738—1750, upon which is painted a view of Redcliff Church. Mr. Fry has two sets of nine tiles each, with the picture of a cat and a dog, and Mr. Willett a copy of Hogarth's "March to Finchley," on a panel composed of seventy-two tiles.

Thomas Heath introduced Delft-ware into Staffordshire towards 1710. *Shaw* tells us how he contrived a new mixture of clays from the coal measures. He describes a dish made by this potter, "which was one of a set manufactured as specimens of the new kind of ware."

Though the author mistakes the white enamel for a dip of white clay, the description is so accurate, that there can be no doubt as to the piece being English Delft. "The upper surface is tolerably even; but the under surface is spotted with minute holes, and exhibits the coarse material of the body." The same peculiarity is to be noticed upon the back of nearly all the dishes coming from Holland; the cause is, that while the inside of the dish is formed on a mould, with a bat of clay carefully smoothed over the surface, the outside has to be cut and turned, thereby exposing all the small holes that may exist in the bulk of the clay; and as the glaze does not penetrate them, after the firing these perforations remain and are increased in size. This was considered such a drawback by the Staffordshire potters that, as we have already observed, they did not attempt to enamel the backs of their dishes, but merely glazed them with lead. In that manner are made those huge dishes representing: Adam and Eve under the tree of knowledge (about the only Scriptural subject which was ever a favourite one with the English Potter, and was restricted to the decoration of Delft-ware), King William and Queen Mary, in an endless variety of patterns, Queen Anne, George I., the Duke of Marlborough, and many celebrated personages of the time. The style of painting is not very commendable; the figures are rudely drawn, and heavily patched with blue; sometimes there is a random staining of copper green or a few dashes of yellow, and clouds and trees are daubed on with a rag or a sponge soaked in blue. It seems as though the painter, whose unattractive task was only to follow a foreign model, did not care whether he pleased himself or anybody else. The rims are marked all round with heavy strokes of the brush, in a way that recalls the indentations practised on the edges of the Slip dishes.

This new kind of ware was no doubt very successful, and its production was stimulated by the serious competition the Dutch carried on against the English potters, even upon their own grounds. The dishes representing William and Mary were first made at Lambeth, before being imitated in Staffordshire. We may safely surmise that the quantity of these dishes still in existence come from different manufactories; and although they never bear any names or marks which could assist us in their identification, we may judge from the inequality of the workmanship and materials that they could not all originate from the same place. Upon some of them are represented the equestrian figure of the king, or the royal couple, elaborately designed by a skilled hand, while the others show nothing more than a barbarous outline or the scrolls of a shapeless ornamentation, traced by a rough workman unacquainted with the first principles of his trade. The same observation applies to the bodies and glazes, as fine and brilliant in the first case as they are rude and imperfect in the second. William III. seems to have fostered by all the means in his power the introduction into England of the faïence of his own country. He was wont to make presents of his portrait painted on large dishes; and it was at the suggestion of his ambassador at the Hague, that, according to Horace Walpole, A. Von Hamme came over to establish a factory in London. In an old family at Dartmouth is still preserved one of these dishes, which the king himself gave to one of the ancestors, then mayor of the town, in acknowledgment of services rendered when he landed as Prince of Orange.

We may well ask ourselves the puzzling question, what has become of the immense quantity of English Delft-ware turned out for a century at the twenty factories that were working at Lambeth, and at the numerous pot works of Liverpool and Bristol, where it once was the staple trade of the town? In our days it is with the greatest difficulty that we can pick up a few stray specimens of undoubted British make amongst the crowd of common pieces sent over by the Dutch exporters, from which they are often hardly distinguishable.

We must say that the making of Delft-ware

never interfered in England with the development of local productions, which continued to be made with native materials. Seldom do we find English Delft in pieces of general use in the country; for example, few, if any, tea-pots, mugs, or common jugs are to be met with. It was limited rather to fancy articles, such as decorative tiles, vases, and dessert plates; most of it was no doubt exported to the colonies, and the small quantity that remained was spread all over the country, and is now, with few exceptions, mistaken for Dutch ware.

Delft-ware became so fashionable that the English potters had to apply that name to such substitutes as they could contrive to manufacture. The ware has disappeared a long time ago, but the name has been preserved to this day, and all common crockery is still called *Delf* in many country places. Lane-Delf became the name of the place where stood the several pot-works manufacturing it, but not before the end of the seventeenth century, as it is not marked on the map drawn by Dr. Plot. It was situated between Lane End and Fenton, and at the present time forms part of the last-named town.

Earnest efforts were made to naturalise the stanniferous enamel in the Potteries, but with little success, the result being very unsatisfactory. The glaze is poor and crazes badly; the colours do not approach the liveliness of continental faïence; besides cobalt and manganese, mostly used, we see only copper green and antimony yellow, sparingly employed and without any brilliancy. The process was hardly diversified in its effects. We possess two jugs coated with a stanniferous blue, decorated with white enamel, much in the style of the Nevers faïence, and a teapot which has the same opaque ground, combined with transparent enamels, and fired in the Salt-glaze oven; but specimens of these kinds are seldom met with.

Not only was the ware ill adapted to domestic requirements, but the tin, so largely used in its manufacture, was so expensive a material, that the potters had to tax their ingenuity until they could supply a somewhat similar article more easily and cheaply manufactured. The white dip, invented by *Astbury*, was resorted to, and might have been successful in its application but for the imperfections of the lead glaze, which tinted it deeply with yellow. Nevertheless, the regular earthenware was found so much superior in quality, that in the Potteries the attempts to imitate the foreign Delft were soon abandoned, while dipped or cream-coloured ware, painted in blue, continued to go by the name of *Delft*. The "dip" process, that is to say, the coating of a coarse clay with a fine white one, was still in use at the beginning of the present century; many of the best blue printed dinner services, with Chinese patterns, are made in that way; the breaking of a piece exhibits a coarse body covered with a thin layer of white slip.

Upon the pieces of Lambeth, Liverpool, and Bristol manufacture, inscriptions occur frequently, and although they lack the "naïve" simplicity of the slip ones, many of them are well worth being recorded. They take the form of short mottoes on the earliest pieces:—

"MAY IT BE WELL USED."
"BE MERRY AND WISE."

On shaving dishes:—

"YOUR QUARTER IS DUE."

On a small caudle pot, as a wish:—

"BOY."

A dish destroyed at the fire of the Alexandra Palace was inscribed:—

"EARTH I AM ET IS MOST TRWE,
DESDAN ME NOT FOR SO AR YOU.
JAN. 16TH, 1660. GEORG: AND ELLIZABETH STERE."

Later on we find allusions to political events:—

"PARLIAMENT BOWL FREE WITHOUT EXCISE, 1736," and "GOD GRANT UNITY, 1746."

Upon six dessert plates, each having one line of a verse, we read:—

1. "WHAT IS A MERRY MAN?"
2. "LET HIM DO WHAT HE CAN,"

3. "TO ENTERTAIN HIS GUESTS"
4. "WITH WINE AND MERRY JESTS,"
5. "BUT IF HIS WIFE DO FROWN,"
6. "ALL MERRIMENT GOES DOWN—1738."

On a bowl in the Geological Museum:—

"JOHN UDY OF LUXILLION
HIS TIN WAS SO FINE
IT GLIDERED THIS PUNCH BOWL
AND MADE IT TO SHINE, &c., &c.—1731."

"ONE BOWL MORE AND THEN."

Doggrel verses, all to the same purport, are very varied on the puzzle jugs:—

"HERE GENTLEMEN COME TRY YOUR SKILL
I'L HOULD A WAGER IF YOU WILL
THAT YOU DON'T DRINK THIS LIQUOR ALL
WITHOUT YOU SPILL OR LET SOME FALL."

"FROM MOTHER EARTH I TOOK MY BIRTH
THEN FORMD A JUG BY MAN
AND NOW STAND HERE FILLD WITH GOOD CHEER
TASTE OF ME IF YOU CAN."

"IF THIS BE YE FIRST THAT YOU HAVE SEEN
I'LL LAY THE WEAGER WHICH YOU PLEASE TO PAY
THAT YOU DON'T DRINK THIS LIQUOR ALL
WITHOUT YOU SPILL OR LET SOME FALL."

"WITHIN THIS CAN THERE IS GOOD LIQUOR
'TIS FIT FOR PARSON OR FOR VICAR
BUT HOW TO DRINK AND NOT TO SPILL
WILL TRY THE UTMOST OF YOUR SKILL."

This is an example of friendly inscriptions on presentation pieces:—

"JOSEPH SWADELL.
WHEN YOU THIS SEE REMEMBER ME
AND BEAR ME IN YOUR MIND
LET ALL THE WORLD SAY WHAT THEY WILL
SPEAK OF ME AS YOU FIND.—1774."

We might multiply quotations, but the above will suffice to show that the Delft potter was very prolific in his poetical lucubrations.

So many counterfeits of foreign ware were made in England as to compel us to acknowledge that, as a rule, English potters were in many instances not over scrupulous as to the way in which they tried to palm off their productions as something different from what they really were. Thus Stone-ware and faïence were at first styled Porcelain; at the same time that English ware was made to imitate that which came from abroad, the latter was sold as home-made. It is also well known that no sooner did some ingenious potter originate a new process or style, and had endeavoured to protect it by affixing his mark, than these marks were pirated in a shameless manner.

Were it not that English Delft had its halcyon days, which cannot be ignored, this chapter ought never to have been written for a book whose special purpose is to point out what was original in the early Ceramic Art of England. In some cases, out of a mere imitation a particular style may develop itself; by degrees it frees itself from leading strings, and then runs freely on a new course; but it was not so with the tin-glazed ware of British manufacture; never was it raised to a very high level, nor did it even attempt to leave the track of a spiritless imitation. The best Liverpool pieces are nothing after all but copies of the Dutch faïence, and would be indistinguishable from their models but for the English inscriptions and a certain clumsiness of execution. Those who manufactured them have left their names in many documents of the time, but by no means the impress of individual genius upon their works; nor did they bequeath to their successors the least discovery or improvement for which any credit can be given to them.

CHAPTER V.

THE BROTHERS ELERS AND THE STAMPED WARE.

THE BROTHERS ELERS COME FROM HOLLAND. — SOME ACCOUNT OF THEIR FAMILY.—JOHN PHILIP PROBABLY THE POTTER OF THE TWO.—BRADWELL WOOD AND DIMSDALE. —THE RED WARE.—METAL DIES USED TO STAMP THE ORNAMENTS.—BLACK WARE.—THE IMITATIONS.— TESTS FOR IDENTIFICATION.—THE WORD PORCELAIN APPLIED IN THAT TIME TO OPAQUE WARE.—INTRODUCTION OF SALT GLAZING.—DEEP SECRECY PRESERVED IN THE MANUFACTORY.—ASTBURY AND TWYFORD DISCOVER THE SECRETS.— THE ELERS LEAVE STAFFORDSHIRE.— JOHN PHILIP JOINS THE CHELSEA GLASS-WORKS. — HE SETTLES IN DUBLIN.—THE WORKS OF ASTBURY AND OTHER IMITATORS. —PORTOBELLO WARE.

THE ELERS.

WHAT the Moors of Spain effected for the improvement of the potter's art in Italy, and what subsequently the Italians did in France (as it has now been ascertained), for the introduction of a new kind of pottery, which was to develop itself there into so many varieties, the Brothers *Elers* did for the advancement of earthenware in Staffordshire. The uneducated butter-pot makers and tilewrights were just beginning to feel the first stirrings of an ambition to improve their coarse productions, when the *Elers* came among them, bringing new ways and new tools, and, above all, their taste for beauty and refinement; such a feeling, hitherto unknown in the district, was in itself sufficient to give an impetus to the latent desire for perfection, without impairing the native originality.

From Holland the Brothers *Elers* seem to have followed the fortunes of the Prince of Orange, and to have come in his train to England in 1688. They were of a noble family of Saxony. Mr. Jewitt *(Life of Josiah Wedgwood)* gives their complete genealogy, but it will be sufficient for our purpose to relate that their father had been Ambassador to several courts of Europe, and that during his term of office as Burgomaster of Amsterdam, he is said to have harboured in his house the royal exile, Henrietta Maria. His two sons, our potters, were John Philip and David; the Elector of Mentz and Queen Christina stood godfather and godmother to the former.

The earliest mention of the name of Elers in this country is found in the Parliamentary Records of the House of Commons; at the date of January, 1680, we see that an engrossed bill for the naturalisation of Peter Elers and others was read a third time, with the resolution "that the bill do pass, and the title be an Act for the naturalisation of Peter Elers and others aliens born." But what relationship existed between this worthy and the two brothers who make the subject of this chapter, we have so far been unable to ascertain.

The date of their arrival in Staffordshire is somewhat uncertain; nor is it known whether William III. continued to extend his patronage to them beyond granting a pension of £300 to their sister. David set up as a merchant, and opened an earthenware shop in London. Was it in the course of his business transactions that he became acquainted with the peculiar advantages offered by Staffordshire for the establishment of a potting manufactory, and was it in that way that the brothers decided to settle on the spot? Or, rather, was it that on coming to England they at once sought the acquaintance of *Dwight*, himself of Dutch extraction, then the leading man of the trade, and in this matter did they act on his advice? *Dwight*, during his stay in Chester, had experimented upon all the clays in the neighbourhood, and no one better acquainted than he with the advantages to be found in the locality could have directed their attention to the remote spot on which they ultimately settled. In 1698 they had already been long at work. Dr. Martin Lister speaks about the red-ware made "by the two Dutchmen brothers who wrought in Staffordshire, and were not long since at Hammersmith." From this we may infer that they were occasionally together in London; but it is probable that while David was selling the ware at his shop in the "Poultry," John Philip was manufacturing it at Bradwell Wood. Indeed, when his son, *Paul Elers*, writes to *Wedgwood* in 1777 about his father, he seems to claim for him alone the honour of having been the first potter in England, directing that under his portrait should be engraved "*Johannes Philipus Elers, Plastices Britannicæ Inventor*" (Miss Meteyard, "*Life of Wedgwood*").

Bradwell Wood is at the present day as lonely a spot as it was in the time of the *Elers*. It lies some distance from the road leading from Wolstanton to Burslem, and a farm-house is the only building on the place. Dimsdale, where the *Elers* stored and sold their productions, is about a mile distant. It is a timbered building of the Elizabethan period, half manor, half farm-house, with a small pool of water in the front, and encircled with clumps of old trees. In the interior a very dilapidated wainscoted room is all that remains of what may have been in the past a noble building; and in that case, if they did really inhabit the hall, the aristocratic potters found there a home befitting their station. At this moment, when the newly-discovered telephone is used so extensively, it is curious to recall the story that the two places had been connected together for convenience sake by a speaking tube made of clay pipes, through which a conversation could be carried on.

There, ready to hand, was to be procured the red clay they wanted for their best work, the ware which was to be the first step towards the imitation of Oriental hard pottery, called by them red porcelain, "for which," says Shaw, "they mixed one part of the Bradwell red clay and four parts of the Hill Top clay." Numbers of hands already trained to the common drudgery of potting were also available on the spot. No doubt this was of great assistance to the new comers, and yet we shall see further on how much they distrusted such helpers as they were obliged to employ.

Industrial art is constantly influenced by circumstances which create fresh wants. It has often been related how the French faïence owes its development to the ruinous war with Holland; the nobility, called upon to contribute to its cost, had to sell their family plate to eke out the failing resources of the king. The potters of Rouen and other places supplied a new kind of earthenware, which, although moderate in price, was not unworthy of having a place upon the table or dresser. When tea was introduced into England, its use at once became so general that cups and teapots could not be imported from China in sufficient quantities; and this new want spreading among all classes of society, a powerful impulse was given to the production of a more delicate and refined sort of ware than that which had been manufactured before for common purposes. The *Elers* found at once scope for displaying their art in the imitation of the dainty little vessels then thought indispensable for brewing the costly beverage, and their red tea-pots and cups found a ready market, at very high prices.

The *Elers* red-ware is a dense and semi-vitrified body, which chemically differs only from porcelain by its lack of translucency. Professor Church gives its hardness as about 5 on the mineralogical scale, and its density as ranging between 2·3 and 2·41. The fineness of the paste is due to the careful levigating and sifting of the natural clay, and its hardness to the high degree of firing to which it was submitted. The colour of the body is of a lighter tint than that of the red-ware made by other makers, and the pieces are especially remarkable for the neat and skilful way in which they were turned on the lathe. Very peculiar is their style of ornamentation, and, however simple and unpretentious in its character, it can be said to have little resemblance to anything done before. It was derived from the recollection of some Japanese or Chinese pieces, imitated, but not actually copied, and so became a style of its own. Rigorous reproduction was certainly not the aim the *Elers* had in view when they produced their red tea-pots, which had nothing Oriental in them but their outward look, for they did not use any of the means which would have conduced to a close imitation, not even the pressing and moulding which are always employed by the Chinese for those pieces which are regarded as having been their models. The raised designs that sparingly decorate the smooth ground were obtained by means of small metal dies sunk in the shape of a flower or a leaf. On the surface, delicately lined over and finished on the wheel, a little lump of wet clay was applied at the place where a relief was intended, and stamped in the same way as the impression of a seal is taken upon wax. The excess of clay round the outlines was then carefully scraped off with a tool, and

FIG. 27. ELERS WARE.—COLL. L. S.

the flowers and leaves were connected together with stems made by hand, so that with the same tools the pattern might be greatly varied. The impressions sometimes represent small figures bearing a strong German character in their design (Fig. 27). Thus we have: the four quarters of the globe; a lady holding a flower, or a huntsman with his gun; but most frequently the ornamentation consists of rosettes, scrolls, or "entrelacs," quite typical in their arrangement. The handles and spouts are plain, and were made by hand. The articles produced by the *Elers* were very simple, and, so far as we know, restricted to tea-ware (Fig. 28). We never came across a single piece of red-ware which was merely ornamental, and which could at the same time with certainty be ascribed to them.

FIG. 28. ELERS WARE.—STOKE MUSEUM.

Though stamping on clay had been commonly used centuries before, on the Samian ware for instance, which was also made of fine red clay, well turned and impressed with seals; on the German grès Stone-ware, and even upon some early English pieces; yet the *Elers*' way of using the tools was very different, and the effect does not recall to the mind any of the above-mentioned potteries. In the Hanley Museum are still preserved a few of these dies (Fig. 29), and also some brass moulds in use at the same period for making spoons and other small pieces.

FIG. 29. BRASS DIE.

A black body made from a mixture of "red clay and oxide of manganese," is said to have been manufactured by the *Elers*, imitated by their successors, and perfected by *Wedgwood* in his black basalt. Of this we have not seen any authentic

FIG. 30. BLACK WARE.—HANLEY MUSEUM.

specimens, but in the aforesaid museum are two teapots of a dead black clay, stamped with seals, and showing the characteristic hawthorn flowers, or vine leaves (Fig. 30). They were presented by Enoch Wood, who knew them to be the work of *Twyford* (one of their imitators), as the label attached to the pieces and written in his own hand testifies. Genuine pieces of *Elers* ware are now exceedingly scarce; but imitations are very numerous, and these are constantly mistaken for real specimens. They continued to be made long after the brothers had left the country. Thus, Shaw mentions the indenture, dated 1750, of one J. Fletcher, who was apprenticed to *J. Taylor*, "to handle, and stick legs to the red porcelain." The identification becomes sometimes difficult when we have to deal with some of these jugs or teapots, which, bearing the same branch of Chinese blossoms, were later on manufactured in so many places; but we may give the following as the results of our observations:—First, seldom, if ever, did the *Elers* produce anything of large dimensions; the most authentic pieces are of a very small size, and the body of the original pieces is so dense that it can be cut upon the lapidary's wheel and receive the polish of a hard stone. Next, the decoration is confined principally to lines and bands sharply turned on the lathe, accompanied with a few flowers or small scrolls stamped in relief with the seal. Lastly, in no case do they show any part that has been pressed in a mould. Spouts and handles modelled into ornamental shapes, such as are to be seen on many pieces which otherwise possess all the peculiarities of the *Elers* ware, are always a sign that these are the works of one of their successors (Fig. 31). As to the pseudo-Chinese marks, these are to be found on the imitations as well as upon the originals, and cannot in any way be relied upon as guides to identification.

Unfortunately, no fragments have ever, to our knowledge, been dug out to enlighten us either upon this red ware or upon any other ware the *Elers* may have manufactured. Tradition has it that they carried away and buried all their imperfect pieces in a distant place. In an expedition

FIG. 31. ELERS STYLE, MADE BY THEIR SUCCESSORS.—SODEN SMITH COLL.

to the site of their works which we made in company with Mr. T. Hulme, of Burslem, we found the excavation where they obtained their red clay, but all the diggings we attempted for "vouchers" were completely fruitless, and the oldest people engaged upon the place told us that they did not remember any fragments of pottery having ever been turned out.

In Germany, a few years later, *Bottcher* was making what he also called Red Porcelain; its finest specimens were, as it is well known, unglazed, and finished by cutting, polishing, and engraving. The *Elers* ware can be treated in the same manner, and we have ourselves tried the experiment with complete success. The outward likeness between the two productions is probably fortuitous; at all events there can be no confusion between them, as the German red pieces are pressed, the ornaments being obtained by moulding instead of stamping. As to the name of Red Porcelain being applied to both, it should be remembered that at that time all Oriental ware, whatever its kind or colour, was called porcelain, and these varieties did not purport to be imitations of the translucent ware which we now call porcelain, but only of the fine red pottery imported from China and Japan. Furthermore, we hear of *Dwight* describing his "grès" Stone-ware as "grey porcelain," and porcelain is also the name given by *Place* to his mottled-ware.

The etymology of the word cannot be said to have been very satisfactorily traced, and numerous and far-fetched are the speculations about it. Not the least curious is that of Dr. Johnson, generally so cautious in his assertions, who gives it as coming from the French "Pour cent ans," because it was a common belief that the materials for making it had previously to be buried for a hundred years. Another strange derivation is the one from the name of King Porcena; tradition says that in his endeavours to avoid being poisoned, he used some cups made of a certain substance which would not hold poison without breaking. It is well known that for a long time all vessels coming from the East were popularly credited in Europe with the same astonishing property, hence the name of Porcena's ware or Porcellena! What we know is, that the word was used in a general way before being restricted to translucent ware.

Some doubts have been raised about the introduction of Salt-glaze into Staffordshire, and as to the making of the white and thin Stone-ware, to which we shall hereafter devote one chapter. It is all the more interesting to know the truth about this question, as we cannot help considering Salt-glaze, or, as it is sometimes called, Crouch-ware, as the most essentially English of all the potteries produced in England. Tales have been circulated which attribute to a local man the invention of glazing with salt. They say that an earthenware pot filled with salt water was left on a kitchen fire, and that the brine boiled over the sides of the pot, which when cold was found to have been glazed by the vapours. *Palmer*, of Bagnall, we are further told, saw it and availed himself of the discovery. It is not possible to discuss seriously the probability of such an incident having ever occurred, for the silicate can only be produced in a closed oven heated to a very high temperature, so that story has to be set aside, to take its place among the many fanciful tales which abound in ceramic lore. In the dialogue given by Ward in his "*History of Stoke-upon-Trent*," we see that the question of the *Elers* having been the first to make Salt-glaze was a common topic of conversation on the ale benches. Much has been done, we are sorry to say, with a view of depriving the foreigners of what credit they are entitled to for laying down the rudiments of a new art, which was to be the starting point of all the improvements made in the pottery of the country. Now that we are able to look back impartially on this controversy, we can safely conclude that they were not only the creators of that special process, but also that they must at once have brought it to perfection.

In favour of the contrary opinion, Shaw ("*History of the Staffordshire Potteries*") brings forward many arguments, all of them far from conclusive. He contends that, for a long time previous, the Staffordshire potters ought to have been acquainted with Salt-glazing, from the knowledge they had of what Dr. Plot calls "kelp," and describes as being the "'Fucus Maritimus,' which in the Isle of Thanet is burned to ashes, put into vessels, and carried over to Holland, with which they glaze all their earthenware." Here Shaw falls into a rather ludicrous mistake for a chemist. The ashes he mentions are the alkalis used in the composition of stanniferous enamel, and not at all the salt employed for the glazing of Stone-ware by evaporation. He also states that he heard from the builders who pulled down the last of the ovens left by the *Elers*, that it was a common biscuit oven, having nothing of the appliances necessary to fire Salt-glaze. We need hardly say that this was probably the one in which they fired their red-ware; the others, erected for different purposes, were, no doubt, demolished a long time before, becoming useless when glazing with salt was completely abandoned.

Had any systematic digging been carried out on the *Elers'* ground, the fragments discovered would at once have settled the question. But an undisputed fact remains, which goes far towards proving that they glazed with salt, and that the practice was quite an unprecedented one in the country. Aitkins *("History of Manchester")* relates that the Burslem potters assembled, eight in number, round the *Elers'* new ovens, to protest against the volumes of smoke they emitted. What other sort of firing could have so created smoke as to frighten the natives, who by this time ought certainly to have been used to the smoke of their own ovens? Salt-glazing, which was at a later date to darken the streets of Burslem in such a way as to render them all but impassable, could alone have taken them by surprise. Mr. Gatty quotes from *Josiah Wedgwood's* papers a note written by his own hand in 1765, containing the particulars supplied to him by a workman named Steel, aged 84, who could remember the Dutchmen at work at Bradwell, and who joined those who ran to the spot, amazed at this unusual mode of firing.

Steel also states that the Salt-glaze ware was first made by the Dutchmen. This should by itself be a sufficient proof. We may add that if Salt-glazing had been discovered and practised by *Palmer* in 1680, Dr. Plott, who wrote in 1686, and goes into such minute particulars, would not have failed to mention it.

It is to be regretted that we have so few documents to help us when we endeavour to ascertain the truth about the potters of that time, but a deep mystery surrounded their researches and their labour; it seems as though they wanted to baffle the curiosity of posterity as well as that of their contemporaries. *Bottcher*, while experimenting upon his new bodies, was actually kept a prisoner in the fortress of Koenigstein, by the Elector of Saxony. The *Elers* seem to have worked in the most profound seclusion, taking every precaution to prevent anyone from prying into their secrets, and being very particular about the sort of people they employed as assistants. Only those who looked dull of understanding were admitted on to the premises; to be an idiot was a recommendation for anyone engaged to turn the wheel while the master was throwing the ware, or to manipulate the clay which had previously been mixed in secrecy. The goods when finished were brought by night from Bradwell to Dimsdale, and only at the latter place were customers allowed to enter.

As might have been expected, so many precautions were certain to excite curiosity. Idiots were not wanting when asked for. Two shrewd men took the trouble to personate the character, and through that artifice *Astbury* and *Twyford* succeeded in witnessing all the manipulations, and mastering most of the secrets. Their conduct, if the tale of the abject deception they kept up for more than two years is true, is not much to their credit, but it is fair to say that *Astbury* afterwards atoned for his duplicity, and redeemed his reputation. Far from remaining satisfied with the stock of knowledge so dishonourably acquired, he prosecuted many experiments, achieved many inventions of his own, and his name will for ever be connected with the great discovery of the value of flint in the earthenware body.

In 1710 the *Elers* are said to have left Staffordshire, and one may well wonder why they ever came into such a place. Aliens, among strange people, who had perhaps never seen a foreigner in their lives; making a secret of all their doings, while everybody in the trade was working in the light of day; selling their teapots in London at a guinea a-piece, while the entire production of other potters hardly averaged four pounds a week; and, above all, retaining probably their refined and aristocratic manners amongst a community who had, so far, advanced but little beyond their primitive roughness; jealousy was rife around them, and life must have been anything but pleasant under these circumstances. They had indeed, nothing to do but go; and away they went, leaving behind them, as at once a pattern and a reproach, their works—a sure guide towards that perfection which their successors endeavoured to attain.

John Philip Elers gave up his business in reduced circumstances, and on his arrival in London became connected with the glass manufactory established in Chelsea in 1676, by Venetians, under the auspices of the Duke of Buckingham. So says Shaw ("*Chemistry of Pottery*"); no other document has ever corroborated the assertion, but in our collection is an *Elers* teapot, decorated all over with scrolls of white and coloured enamels similar to those which are generally used in a glass manufactory; this curious specimen might perhaps be taken as one of their experiments in this new pursuit.

We have always spoken of the brothers jointly in all we have said concerning their life and their works, so adhering to tradition, though we believe John Philip alone was the potter. At the end of their career we find them separated. Again we lose sight of David, but learn from the particulars given to *Josiah Wedgwood* by Edgeworth, that John Philip went to Dublin, where, with the assistance of Lady Barrington, he set up a glass and china shop, and became very prosperous in business. (Miss Meteyard's "*Life of Wedgwood.*")

After their departure, the new ways of potting they had introduced, though kept up in the main, underwent some transformations. Making a compromise between the old style and the new, *Astbury* continued to apply ornaments on the red clay, still impressed with small metal seals, but he used white clay to contrast them with the ground, and glazed them over with galena.

At Shelton, where stood his manufactory, many fragments were discovered a few years ago. They are all pieces of tea and coffee ware, made of the fine red clay, richly glazed and ornamented with white embossments. Among the subjects are the royal arms, the fleur-de-lys, or, more frequently birds and flowers, somewhat different in design from the *Elers'* seals, and far from equalling in finish the perfection of the red porcelain; but neatness of execution seems to have given way to a desire for brightness of colour (Fig. 31). Various

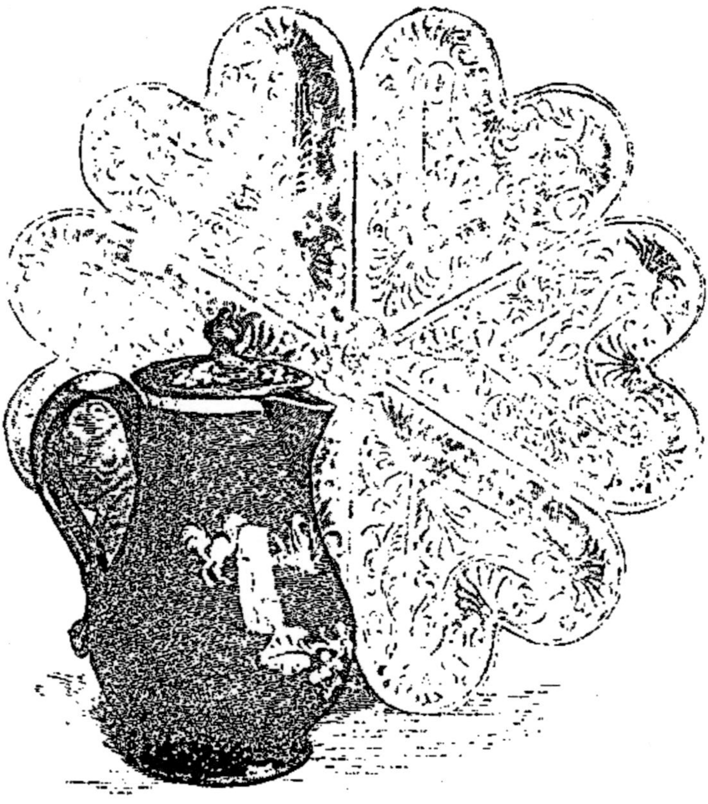

FIG. 31. ASTBURY CREAM JUG AND SWEETMEAT TRAY OF STAMPED WARE.—COLL. L. S.

coloured grounds are chosen to set out the reliefs; upon the shining black clay run white branches of vine; little yellow cocks stand out on the shining red. The red clay is applied in the shape of hawthorn blossoms upon the yellow or buff body, the most elaborate and finely stamped specimens being of a saffron yellow ground, covered with scrolls and leaves of great delicacy. Sometimes we have a would-be Chinese figure; the whole enlivened by touches of flowing and transparent colour, such as are used on the tortoiseshell-ware. The handles and knobs are in all cases of the same clay as the ornaments, and are still made by hand.

For a long time afterwards stamping was used to complete the ware turned on the wheel, whether it was white Salt-glaze, or earthenware of coloured body, glazed with lead. Red porcelain was still made, but how different in quality! We possess a huge red teapot profusely decorated with branches and rosettes done by the old process; it has been silver-mounted, which shows that some value was set upon it, yet it is so coarse in execution that it could not stand comparison with any of the earlier pieces. We have also an identical replica of the small red teapot, preserved at Etruria, as the first piece made by *Wedgwood* during his apprenticeship; but the raised blossoms spread upon it are made in the German way, that is to say, moulded separately and stuck on the surface, and we greatly doubt its being of English origin.

Pottery becoming more popular, its makers took advantage of all the great events of the time. A new sort of ware was made to spread the news of a victory, or to commemorate its glory. In 1727 *Astbury* created the Portobello ware, which had a great run after the expedition of—

> "Admiral Vernon, that brave fellow (who)
> With six ships took Porto-bello."

Dies were sunk in the shape of ships, and whole flotillas were stamped in white on the red tea-ware. In the British Museum is a very fine

FIG. 32. PORTOBELLO WARE.—MR. H. WILLETT'S COLL.

bowl so decorated. On other pieces the full-length figure of the hero is represented, and also a conventional view of the fortifications (Fig. 32). Mr. H. Willett has two different Salt-glaze teapots made in honour of the admiral.

Of *Astbury* and his discoveries a good deal more will be said hereafter. We have only spoken of him here in connection with the stamped-ware, and as being the worthiest successor of the *Elers.* Trained by the foreigners, but soon getting out of the bounds of servile imitation, he altered and improved their fabric into one of genuine English character in all its particulars—manufacture as well as design.

CHAPTER VI.

SALT-GLAZE.

Origin of the White Stone-Ware glazed with Salt.—Salt-Glaze Ovens in Burslem.—The Glaze and its high degree of Firing.—Composition of the Body.—Stamped Ornaments and Brass Moulds.—Mould Cutting.—Casting.—Introduction of Plaster Moulds.—Extension of the Pottery Trade in Staffordshire.—Astbury and the other leading Potters of the Period.—Variety of Shapes and their Originality.—Different processes connected with the Salt-Glaze Ware.—Scratched Blue.—Competition with the German Ware.—Enamelled Salt-Glaze.—Gilding.—Reproduction of China pieces made in Salt-Glaze Ware.—Tiles.—Perforated Pieces.—Localities where Salt-Glaze was Manufactured.

SALT-GLAZE.

HAD we to describe in a few words a piece of the ware which will make the subject of the present chapter, we should say: it is a white earthen vessel, daintily formed, delicately embossed with graceful arabesques or flowers, and which shows, under a pellucid glaze, brightening, but not hiding, the sharpness of the most minute details, a semi-transparence in the thinnest parts of its substance. Would not the description read as if some sort of Porcelain was intended? And yet we only applied it in our mind to English Salt-glaze, the new ware which was once opposed in England to the heavily-made and darkly-coloured earthenware, the brown stone, or the clumsy Delft, heretofore the only fictile productions of the country. With this discovery the potters thought for a time that they could compete with the costly importations from the East; or at least, if complete success was not yet achieved, that they were on the eve of solving the mystery of the Chinese porcelain, the wonder of all Europe, a mystery so difficult to penetrate that for some time it was coupled with the secret of the philosopher's stone. Distant as it was from a perfect imitation, yet the success which attended the appearance of the first specimen of Salt-glaze was immense, and its use suddenly spread all over the kingdom.

In the chapter on Stone-ware, a ware also glazed with salt, we have described the chemical action of the silica of the paste upon the vapours of the soda contained in the common salt, and how by means of its evaporation the glaze is formed upon the ware. We have also said that any clay refractory enough to stand the requisite temperature can from ordinary earthenware be transformed into stone-ware, that is to say, may show a commencement of vitrification all through the texture of the body; a still higher degree of heat could even fuse it into a glass; but in this case the fusion is uncontrollable, and no transparent ware could safely be made out of it. This was one of *Dwight's* difficulties in his experiments for making Porcelain. Even in the Potteries, when the composition of the paste had been settled after protracted experiments, too much fire caused the ware to melt. We have seen many examples of cast-away saggers with all the pieces they contained sticking to each other and sunk at the bottom in a shapeless mass.

The glaze offers this peculiarity, that it does not run and spread like other glazes, but remains in the state of minute drops or granulations; its surface can be compared to leather or orange peel. These particles are more or less conspicuous according to the conditions of the firing. Sometimes, when red lead was added to the salt, the fluidity of the mixture makes them hardly perceptible. Often the gloss is unequally distributed over the pieces; although the saggers in which they were enclosed for protection were pierced with large holes, the vapours of soda did not reach every place in the same proportion, so occasionally one side may be quite dry while the other is highly glazed.

At an early date a sort of white-ware glazed with salt was made in Germany, and thence probably the process was carried into England. We cannot also doubt that *Dwight* made at Fulham a kind of white Stone-ware glazed with salt. But amongst the various productions of other places and other times, nothing calls back to our mind the genuine works of the old English Potter; out of a process certainly known before his days he contrived to create an original style of pottery, for which credit must be given to him. We have no hesitation in saying that, such as it stands now preserved in many diversified examples in the cabinets of the collectors, the thin "Salt-glaze," or the English white Stone-ware which is known under that name, originated in the district where it was so extensively manufactured, viz., the Staffordshire Potteries.

We have already stated upon what grounds the introduction of the process may be attributed to *John Philip Elers;* at all events, it was only a few years after the brothers had settled down at Bradwell, and astonished the inhabitants with their unwonted way of conducting the firing, that Salt-glaze ovens were erected all over the town of Burslem. It is reported that so many factories were at work at that time, that on Saturday mornings, when the fires were at their highest and drawing towards the end, the smoke emitted was so dense as to cause the passer-by to grope his way, as in the midst of the thickest London fog, amongst fumes "not unlike" says the author, "the smoke of Mount Vesuvius." On the scaffolds that surrounded the oven, several men stood opposite the apertures of each of the flues, shovelling the salt into the fire; and every time they fed the fiery mouths, the flames, driving away for a moment the murky smoke, revealed to view the men wrapped in clothes soaked with water, and their faces protected by wet sheets.

No marks, no dates, come to elucidate the

problem of when and by whom the first pieces were made. Here again we are reduced to speculation. Contradictory statements are in existence; we can dismiss some of them on account of their improbability, acknowledging at the same time that something might be learnt from them if we could only understand their real purport, instead of continuing to be misled by the inappropriate terms in which they are worded.

When the attention of collectors was first drawn to these curious and undescribed pieces, they were erroneously called "Elizabethan Ware." We have now made it clear that the mistake arose out of a jug of that manufacture being preserved in Shakespear's House, at Stratford, where it had been known for a long time by the name of "Shakespear's Jug," and which, probably made in the Potteries towards the middle of the last century, had nothing in common with the great poet.

We cannot, knowing the conditions of temperature required for Salt-glazing, place any reliance upon the tradition which attributes its discovery to *Palmer*, of Bagnall, in 1680. The tale, as reported by several authors, says that a servant had left on the fire a pot full of salt-water, and that the brine overboiling, covered the outside of the pot with a bright glaze; a surprising fact which the potter immediately turned to account, and put into practice in his factory. That the glaze should thus be formed in an open place may be considered an utter impossibility, and therefore this long-credited story can be regarded as disposed of.

If it is still a doubtful point whether the *Elers* actually introduced Salt-glazing into Staffordshire, we at all events have proof that this manufacture did not prevail in the Potteries very early in the eighteenth century after they had left the country. From the perusal of the list of the Burslem potters at work between 1710 and 1715, we see that there were only six ovens in the town turning out Stone-ware, and even then no special mention is made of its being glazed with salt; not one potter was making Stone-ware of any sort in Hanley.

It is probable that it was only about that time the Staffordshire potters began to make a fire-resisting body which could stand the required temperature, by mixing the whitish clay found at Shelton with the fine sand of Baddeley Edge, or else the cane marl with the grit from Mow Cop. To these materials were also added, before the discovery of flint, the white clay employed by the pipemakers, and with which were made the first experiments for a white ware. Pipes had been manufactured at Newcastle-under-Lyme, as well as in many other places, years before Dr. Plot visited the Potteries; he describes how *Charles Riggs*, of Newcastle, made them of three different sorts of clays, the best of which was found between Shelton and Hanley Green. Many of these pipes, impressed with the initials of the maker, have been from time to time dug up in quantities; and as they are quite white and well fired, surprise might be felt that the same material had not been turned into good account for the making of pots. The reason is that the lead ore then used for glazing did not allow of any glazed white ware being made, as it turned the whitest biscuit to a dingy yellow tint; but as soon as the colourless glaze obtained with salt was discovered, pipe-clay became the basis of many new compounds.

In the Potteries district no materials were employed at first but those procured on the spot; with the marl, the clays from the coal measures, and the sand also found in the locality, they made the "buff" ware; for white ware they had the pipe-clay and the grit excavated from the Mow Cop strata; the requisite salt was obtained from the neighbouring mines; thus it can fairly be called a genuine Staffordshire production. We shall hereafter show how its shapes and decorations may also set up an unquestionable claim to indigenous originality.

We have all reasons to suppose that a "buff" body was first attempted with the same clay as had been employed long before for common stone pots, and that the use of white pipe-clay was then confined to such small raised ornaments as were sparingly applied on the surface; the ware did not become quite white until it had passed through many successive improvements all aiming in that direction. The earliest kind was of a greenish tint, and was called "Crouch-ware." That term, which has puzzled more than one, comes from the name of the white Derbyshire clay; long before being used for Salt-glaze, it had been employed at Nottingham to make crucibles and glass pots, and under

FIG. 33. SALT-GLAZE WITH ELERS ORNAMENTS.—COLL. L. S.

the name of "Crouch clay" it figures in several old documents.

Most of the early pieces bear such a striking resemblance to the red porcelain of the *Elers*, in potting as well as in ornamentation, that it is difficult not to ascribe the same origin to both wares (Fig. 33).

The Crouch-ware is of a dense paste; if not

quite so hard as the red porcelain, it is because the ferric oxide contained in the latter increases its vitreousness. The shapes, neatly formed, are equally well finished on the lathe; and a pressed part is never added to them, excepting perhaps occasional feet or claws, impressed in the "pitcher" moulds of one single piece, which went by the name of "thumb moulds."

In his MS. notes, *Josiah Wedgwood* relates that the *Elers* introduced moulds of plaster of Paris. We cannot implicitly trust this assertion, as it is not corroborated by any known example; on the contrary, from all the specimens that have come under our notice, and other collateral proofs, we can deduce the fact that they did not employ any moulds, either of plaster or terra cotta; they stamped on and did not press separately the applied ornaments, differing in this particular from *Dwight*, who worked by the latter process. We find in his notes mention of a "grey clay to be 'spriged' with white;" the term is still used in our days, and means to stick on the surface the relief taken out of a mould. We shall insist upon the point that in the *Elers* ware all the ornaments are stamped on the piece itself with small metal seals, as can be ascertained by the traces of the impression of the die, the square ground of which is sunk in the clay round the raised subjects. Made in this way, we have many remarkable pieces of buff colour, relieved by rosettes and entwined lines of white clay, not unlike in design the typographic ornaments of the period. The forms are finely turned and finished, and seldom show any defect, but the raised parts have cracked in many places, as though the difficulty of making the two clays agree together had not yet been completely mastered. Enoch Wood's collection was especially rich in specimens of this ware, now so difficult to obtain, and that fact tends to prove that it was made in the Potteries. Pieces of the same description are also found having a wash of white clay in the inside, or even made entirely of the white body; these may safely be attributed to the successors of the *Elers*, who continued to work in their style long after the Dutchmen had left the country.

As the new ware was especially admired on account of its thinness and delicacy, all efforts were made to insure and increase these qualities; spoons, sauce boats, and small trays were manufactured as light as wafers, by means of copper or lead moulds, which acted like our goffering irons, impressing them at one blow on the outer and inner surfaces (Fig. 34). The notion of such moulds was no doubt derived from the usual brass seals; they have now become very scarce, yet some of them are preserved in the Geological Museum and in the Hanley Institute. But the use of copper moulds was limited to very small pieces, and additional means had to be resorted to, such as casting and pressing. Pieces of large dimensions had to be cast in "pitcher" or terra-cotta moulds.

Here we shall describe the peculiar process by which models and moulds were made; instead of modelling the form in relief as we should now-a-days, it was hollowed out of several pieces of

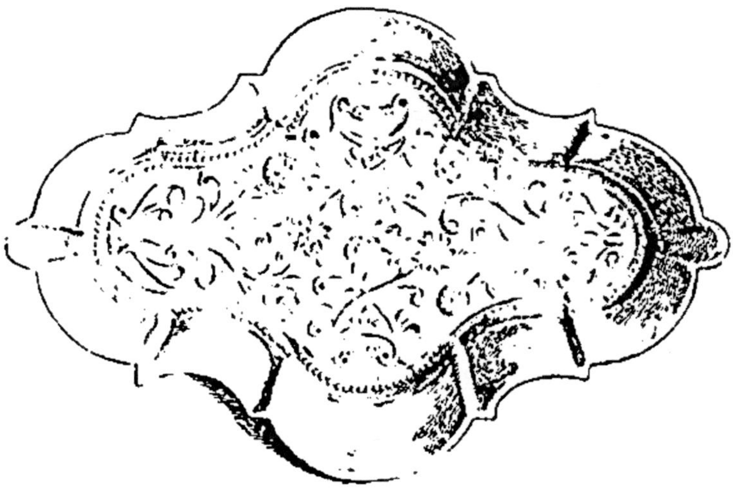

FIG. 34. SMALL TRAY, STAMPED IN A BRASS MOULD.—COLL. L. S.

native gypsum, which formed the different sections of the intended mould; after they had been graven and sunk with complicated patterns of flowers and scrolls, a proof was taken, and, being fired in the oven, it became what was called the "block;" upon this block an unlimited number of clay moulds could be made, all of which preserved the sharpness of the original work.

Sometimes they were fired, thus becoming practically indestructible, but often the clay was only dried. An old workman of Hanley was, a few years ago, still casting very neat pieces in moulds of dry clay, by what he called the old process.

Many of the old routine ways have long continued in the Potteries, and have outlived the new-fangled fashions which successively gave way to one another; consequently, from the mere make of a particular specimen, to fix the period to which it belongs is often a matter of guesswork, and in the absence of an inscribed date, never goes beyond mere probability. We possess an earthenware cream jug, the form of which is divided in eight compartments, with embossed subjects. The mould was constructed on the old system, and the piece, thinly cast and not pressed, has all the characteristics of an early specimen; the little figures, very numerous and varied, are as sharp in detail and quaint in design as on the finest models of Salt-glaze, and the whole is touched up with tortoiseshell colours. Two initials, "H. R.," are scratched under the bottom, and the top has the name of "*John Lucas*" painted in blue. This shows the jug to be a presentation piece, and we may take it to be the work of an old workman, who was pleased to revive for once the best fashions of his younger days; otherwise, were we to consider it a regular production of the period, when finding it, to our amazement, dated as late as 1790, nothing would remain for the collector but to declare his utter incapability to distinguish such ware from what was manufactured in the beginning of the same century.

By examining the style of embossments of the Salt-glaze ware, we perceive at once how well the

FIG. 35. SALT-GLAZE SHELL TEA-POT.—COLL. L. S.

decoration is contrived to allow of its being conveniently carved in the hollow shell of the mould; each section has a separate subject, and the seams existing between the sections, which are the great trouble of the potter, who vainly tries to conceal them by any other means, have been made use of in the composition as partition lines which divide it into panels. The subjects were always selected with the view of affording the greatest facility of execution. For instance, the "mould cutters," as they were called, found the "pecten" shell, with its many ribs, especially appropriate to their style of carving, so they brought it to bear in an endless variety of combinations, and with it are associated such small foliage and lines as can be conveniently engraved in the mould with a single stroke of the gouge (Fig. 35). When a piece was intended to be produced by casting, the model was seldom made of a round shape; for these latter, turning, with application of stamped ornaments, was generally preferred; for a cast piece, pentagonal and lobed shapes were contrived, and the seams of the moulds in such cases were, as we have already remarked, used to divide the sections from each other by a raised line. It has been advanced that the earliest models were taken from silver plate pieces. The fact is patent with respect to some of the china made at Bow, Chelsea, and Worcester, but does not apply to Salt-glaze ware. This had a style of its own, which in no way recalls the "repoussé" or chased work of the silversmiths, and the likeness they show to some old silver plate does not go beyond the general appearance which appertains to all works of contemporary times.

In the "pitcher" moulds the ware was not pressed, but cast; the process of casting consisted in filling the mould with diluted clay or slip, then pouring it out, leaving a thin coat of clay on the surface; as soon as it began to dry the operation was repeated, and each time the coating increased in thickness. When the required strength had been obtained the whole was placed before the fire, and by desiccation the piece separated from the mould; it was then ready to be garnished with the handles, spouts, or claws, which had been separately cast in the same way. The pieces made in "terra cotta" or brass moulds are the most ancient, and are far superior, in sharpness of detail and style of execution, to the comparatively modern ones cast in plaster moulds. These latter were easily deteriorated, and as they were still used after having been quite worn out, very poor stuff was produced as soon as they superseded the "pitcher" moulds. It was not until 1750 that *Ralph Daniel*, of Burslem, brought back, from a porcelain manufactory he had visited in France, the first mould in plaster of Paris; the innovation was adopted at once by the other potters of his town, and it afforded great facilities for quickness of production, but often at the expense of neatness and quality. At the same date "pressing," that is to say, moulding with a thick lump of clay, began to be substituted for casting, and the daintily embossed pieces soon disappeared altogether.

But to return to the introduction of Salt-glaze into the Potteries, and the influence it had upon the general trade of the country, we must once more call to mind the fact that pottery in that district had so far been only a modest craft, by which the master could in his single thatched hovel average only a produce of the value of four or five pounds a week, out of which all expenses had to be paid. Several common hands were employed at each place; but the best

FIG. 36. EARLY SALT-GLAZE TEA-POY.—LADY SCHREIBER'S COLL.

workman who could throw, turn, and handle, had to divide his time, and work for two or three factories in the same week.

The effect of the introduction of this new white ware was to turn a small trade into a large industry. The one oven of each potter had to be increased in size, the small quantity of goods that could be turned out of it could no longer answer the demand, and soon, to the astonishment of the inhabitants of Shelton, *R. & J. Baddeley* erected four ovens in a row behind their manufactory. Instead of being limited to the precarious dealings carried on with the adjoining counties, the ware began to be carted away to all parts of England. Business connections were established with distant towns.

Fig. 37. Salt-glaze Tea-pot.—Coll. L. S.

Travellers were sent off with a load of goods, to sell the stock and take further orders; but the way of trading was still very primitive. "When they came home," says Shaw, "after having disposed of their ware, they simply emptied the money bag of its contents, without rendering any account of their transactions."

Notwithstanding the cheapness of labour at the time, the care bestowed upon these delicate little pieces made them rather expensive in comparison with the common earthen pots, and we think that Salt-glaze remained for a long time the highest class of ware, and was paid for accordingly. Nothing can excel in delicacy some of the diminutive four-lobed teapots, resting on three minute claws and embossed all over with shells, oak leaves, and acorns (Fig. 37). Evidently destined as a present to a lady of taste and refinement, it is difficult to decide whether they can be called toys, gimcracks, or teapots. Though the size of the ovens had been enlarged, and the weekly production greatly increased, little of it was kept for home use, but the ware was sent away to be sold everywhere to well-to-do people. In my experience of old pot hunting in Staffordshire, I have hardly found any Salt-glaze pieces in the cottages; all I have gathered together, though mostly manufactured in the Potteries, came from other counties. I may, however, say that they stood more chances of being destroyed than any other ware, being so fragile, and liable to break in hot water. An immense quantity must have been exported into Holland; it is now returned to us by the Dutch dealers; and, strange as it may appear, it is from that source that the best specimens have come to enrich the English collections.

Astbury and *Twyford* took the lead in the manufacture of Salt-glaze, the former employing the Bideford pipe-clay and the Devon and Dorset clays, which, from the ports whence they were obtained, were called Chester clays. They therefore departed from the custom of using local materials only. *Astbury* washed with these clays the inner surface of his buff Stone-ware, and with them made also a white stone body, which he still further improved by making ground flint the principal ingredient of it, an invention to which we shall have hereafter to refer more amply.

FIG. 31. RALPH SHAW WARE.—(Coll. L. S.

Thomas Billing, in 1722, took out a patent "for making the most refined earthenware, of a nature and composition not only transparent, but so perfect in its kind as, contrary to the nature of all other earthenwares, to resist almost any degree of heat." The specification of transparency here indicates a sort of Salt-glaze, while the inventor was trying to overcome the objection put forth against its general use, by boasting, like many others, of having found the means of remedying that imperfection.

Ralph Shaw, of Burslem, took out a patent, in 1732, for a chocolate ware, which was white inside, and the upper surface of which was covered with alternate coats of brown and white, scratched in with lines and flowers. The invention was applied to Stone-ware glazed with salt; we give (Fig. 38) a sketch of a bowl of that ware, now become exceedingly scarce. We shall have occasion to refer to him more fully in the next chapter.

Dr. Thomas Wedgwood was the principal potter of Burslem at that time, making various kinds of ware besides Salt-glaze. To him, in 1731, was apprenticed *Aaron Wood*, who attained to the greatest reputation as "block cutter and mould maker," and enjoyed the privilege of working in a room by himself, where he remained locked up all the day by his employer. He was to work for no one else but his present master, and the master in his turn promises in his agreement that he will "employe him in, but himself only." Some of the moulds made by *A. Wood* have been preserved, and bear his name scratched in the paste; one of them is in the South Kensington Museum.

Thomas & John Wedgwood established themselves at Burslem as makers of white Stone-ware before 1740, and introduced many improvements in its manufacture by experimenting on the liability of the various clays to crack or break in the firing. Their enterprising spirit was generally censured, and considered little short of extravagance. They erected a spacious manufactory covered with tiles, while all the others were still covered with thatch, and they had three ovens built on their premises.

The brothers *Baddeley*, who at the same time had four ovens erected in a row behind their workshops, made elegant white Stone-ware, including fruit baskets, and bread or sweet trays, cast in moulds, and exhibiting ornaments on both sides.

Aaron Wood and *William Littler*, employing for the first time the oxide of cobalt as a ground, made the first blue Salt-glaze, which was said to resemble the finest "*lapis lazuli.*"

Many other names might be added to this list, but the above are sufficient to show how the potters tried to rival each other, and bring out some improvement of their own in their specialities. Unfortunately, however varied and distinct the specimens are, very few of them can safely be attributed to any of these makers in particular, so little care has been taken to preserve the traditions by which not long ago many might have been identified.

The imagination of the Staffordshire "block cutters" was very fertile in quaint devices; for instance, in the case of simple tea-pots, they seem to have exhausted every conceivable shape. We have tea-pots that are globular, elliptic, octagonal, square, and oblong; others that are formed like two or more shells; and others again that are heart-shaped. All sorts of animals or figures are used; a squirrel, or a bird, a bear with its cub, and a Bacchus astride on his cask. This last was probably made by, or for, *Thomas Bacchus*, of Lane End, a potter, who married *Astbury's* widow.

New shapes were required to set forth in all its originality the new Salt-glaze ware, which was from the first manufactured with materials so different from those which had been used before; public taste soon got tired of globular shapes turned on the wheel, and having a uniform profile, either left plain or insufficiently diversified by applications of meagre flowers or leaves. The secret of the manufacture of white ware could not long be kept amongst a few, but soon became public property, and the competing potters had to exercise their wits in bringing out striking novelties, endeavouring in that way to outdo each other. The imagination of modellers on their mettle gave vent to all sorts of inventions, verging sometimes on extravagance, and the process of casting lately introduced permitted them to execute their most complicated conceptions. There was no natural object, no impracticable representation of animal or figure that was not thought fit to be turned into a tea-pot. A camel, for instance, could not at first sight be considered a very promising subject for that purpose. Perhaps on this account it was often preferred, and the difficulties surmounted in different ways. Sometimes the camel is represented in its naturalistic shape, or else the model combines in a highly conventional style the ribs of the shell pattern with the general outlines of the kneeling animal (Fig. 39). We know not

FIG. 39. CAMEL TEA-POT.- WILLETT COLL.

fewer than five different shapes of these camel tea-pots. When squirrels, bears, cats, and other animals were intended, they were in all cases made ornamental with scrolls or flowers embossed all over, thus avoiding the ludicrous effect always evinced by a too realistic production (Fig. 40).

Large numbers of Salt-glaze tea-pots were made in the shape of a house, sometimes having the royal arms over the door, and a sentry on each side, but more frequently reproducing some private dwelling. Considering how proud a man is when he builds a house of his own, and how every allusion to the subject pleasantly tickles his vanity, may not such a piece have been thought an appropriate present to offer to a friend on such an occasion? What gives weight to our supposi-

FIG. 40. SQUIRREL TEA-POT.—COLL. L. S.

tion with regard to these numerous tea-pots is, that they are never made to represent a curious building, or an ambitious palace, but the square and common-place home of a well-to-do Englishman.

Without asserting that every Staffordshire teapot was intended to convey a special meaning, we must admit, from many examples, that people in olden times were often prompted to embody their thoughts in a tangible shape—what they could not write they expressed in a graphic form. Lovers offered to each other a symbolical tea-pot in the shape of a heart; for the man of politics there was the tea-pot commemorating a successful election, or a great victory like the taking of Portobello by Admiral Vernon; and we are not at all sure that the Bacchus tea-pot was not a sarcastic present to an habitual drunkard, forestalling in this forcible way the teachings of "teetotalism."

Sometimes the artist gives vent to his fancy, and models by hand a little group, which will not be reproduced. Such is the interesting example in Mr. Willett's collection, of a lady seated in the church pew with her two grown up sons by her side, or the quaint group of two figures we have etched for our first edition.

It is surprising to find such a piece as this last one, evidently the fruit of a whimsical imagination, to which no special purpose can be attributed, made at a time when modelling was confined to the raised ornaments which were sparingly used to complete smoothly-turned shapes, and when fancy could only exercise itself on the commonest articles of daily use. We may ask ourselves whether this dignified lady and gentleman, attired in their Sunday clothes, and resting upon their homely settle, are the portraits of "the Squire and his wife," or merely the fanciful creation of the maker's inventive mind? If the latter, the choice of the subject may be said to be quite on a level with its primitive execution, and the style of modelling had indeed to undergo a great and rapid change before the modellers of the Potteries could produce the varied, ingenious, and clever figures which were made a few years afterwards.

We can see by the awkwardness of this group that it was not a common practice at that time to turn out a work of this kind; the costumes of the figures refer it to the period of slip dishes, and it suggests to us the idea of *Thomas Toft* trying his hand at sculpture.

Perhaps the best representative piece of the Salt-glaze fabrication, the one where the qualities and faults of the ware are the most forcibly exemplified, is the large mug engraved in the first edition of this work; one copy of the same mug was found with the other pieces discovered in the old Fulham Works, and for that reason had been by some considered as being of *Dwight's* manufacture. Such an example is sufficient to make us understand how deceptive a style of ornamentation may prove if, by it alone, we try to determine the age of a piece of earthenware! Looking at the profusion of uncouth birds, reptiles, and quadrupeds spread all over the sides of this mug, and the stiff border of nondescript flowers arranged on its base, we could not help surmising that they had been inspired by the illumination of some mediæval MS., and that the quaint work was contemporaneous with the old missals; yet, in the centre has been reproduced a comparatively modern picture by Hogarth; its title, "Midnight Conversation," has been engraved underneath, to prevent any doubt in that respect. The modeller was at no pains to modify his Gothic manner when engaged in imitating the principal features of the well-known composition; it is a free and easy adaptation, and all the personages, notwithstanding their periwigs and tobacco pipes, have a decidedly Byzantine appearance. Could such primitive-looking images have been perpetrated in London after 1750, the date of the publication of Hogarth's engraving, where artists lived surrounded by the best works of the time?

It can for several reasons be attributed to Staffordshire; the ware is exactly similar to the Salt-glaze of the Potteries; the subject was there at the time a favourite one. In the Stoke Museum may be seen a large cream-coloured punch bowl, decorated over the glaze with the same "Midnight Conversation," still an adaptation of the original, though painted in a less barbarous manner. But the last proof in support of our supposition is the most decisive; it is the presence on the piece of four coats of arms, three of them belonging to Staffordshire families. *Hales*, baronet, *Leveson-Gower*, *Vane*, and *Bertie*. Another Salt-glaze mug of the same shape and size, but with a different decoration, has in addition to the four escutcheons named above, the cognizances of two other families, also connected with Staffordshire, *Whorewood* and *Granville*. This is in Mr. Willett's collection. Unlike the German Stone-ware which displays

FIG. 41. SALT-GLAZE CUP.—COLL. L. S.

such an abundance of escutcheons that a whole armory is to be found on Rhenish Ceramics, very seldom does the white Stone-ware of England offer any coat of arms, mottoes, or devices belonging to the nobility of the manufacturing counties; the potter does not seem to have ever courted their patronage. However we give here (Fig. 41) another of the rare exceptions to that rule; it is a cup of the early period, which has, besides the Royal arms, those of *Warwick* and *Leveson Gower.*

Tea-ware, sauce-boats, sweetmeat and pickle trays, and such minute articles were the first productions of the improving Potteries, and very great skill was displayed upon the models. We shall mention, as an example, the remarkable sauce-boat belonging to Professor A. Church, upon which the Seven Champions of Christendom are elaborately represented. Purely ornamental pieces soon after began to be manufactured, such

FIG. 42. EARLY SALT-GLAZE SAUCE-BOAT.—HANLEY INSTITUTE.

as spill vases, flower pots, and hanging brackets, but in no case do they exhibit any attempt to imitate a foreign model. They are, on the contrary, striking instances of what can be done with an art which, born on the soil, there gradually develops itself without any extraneous assistance. Table-ware was only attempted much later on; even at the Worcester China Manufactory they avoided in the first years making anything of large size, and some contemporaries expressed their astonishment at the want of enterprise of the English china makers, who had not so far tried to compete with the plates and dishes imported from the East, the only ones that could then be obtained for dinner services.

Amongst the pieces of the late period can be ranged the soup tureens, one of which is now in the Jermyn Street Museum; it bears the date, 1763, and the initials "J. B." scratched at the bottom. These two letters might stand for the name of *John Baddeley*, who was at that time one of the best potters of Staffordshire, and was making ware of precisely the same description; we cannot say positively that it may be considered as his mark, but in support of such a supposition, we can identify the pattern as being the work of *Aaron Wood*, the modeller he employed, and who has signed with his name more than one block belonging to the same set. The design consists of the same basket-work, diaper of dots and conventional leaves, which was so often repeated upon all sorts of table-ware. It is a late piece, and although the ornaments have been sunk in the mould after the old style, the form is thick and coarsely cast; the moulding is no longer finished on the lathe, and the ornaments have lost their sharpness. This soup tureen is by no means an uncommon specimen; we have ourselves seen many similar ones, but in all these the knobs and claws were very different; this might be explained by the fact that pieces of this kind were produced by more than one maker.

The fact that soup tureens were so extensively made is not easily reconcilable with the notion that soup appeared on the table of very few Englishmen of the time, and would show that Salt-glaze was intended for the upper classes. The names under which they are designated in the old accounts is the French word "*terrine*," an earthen basin, which subsequently was altered into tureen. Pickle trays are also described from the French as "*hors-d'œuvre.*"

A collection formed with the view to illustrate all the different kinds of Salt-glaze ware made in Staffordshire during three quarters of a century, would in itself comprise innumerable varieties of pieces and processes, so diversified were the transformations the fabric was made to undergo, from the massive jar, impervious and indestructible, the material of which could not be surpassed for the uses to which it was put, to dainty little cups, the prettiness of which rivals porcelain. Long before Salt-glazing had made its appearance in England, "Grès" Stone-ware had been manufactured in Germany, and brought to a high degree of excellence. There the theme had its origin, but the English potter added to it endless variations. He was the first who attempted to impart to his Stone-ware a lightness of substance and a gloss of surface which could render it fit for all sorts of decorations. Setting aside the brown pieces made in imitation of German ones, of which we have spoken in a previous chapter, we shall try to briefly describe the varieties which would constitute a complete collection of Salt-glaze. These are:—

Ornaments of white clay, stamped with seals, on a buff or white body, in the style of the *Elers*.

Flowers or foliage "sprigged" on the piece, that is to say, made in a separate mould and stuck on with the slip, the stems which join them together being made by hand with a strip of clay.

Thin pieces covered with embossments, made in copper or "pitcher" moulds, in all sorts of picturesque forms, body of greyish or dull yellow colour, glaze dry.

Engine-turned pieces in great variety.

Mixtures of coloured bodies in the style of the Agate-ware.

Combinations of the common red clay with a coating of white Stone-ware, the scratching of the upper coat showing the dark clay underneath in the same way as the Italian *Sgrafiato*.

Pieces made in plaster moulds; white body, thicker in substance and less sharp in execution.

Perforated dishes and basket ware.

Pressed tiles, with landscapes in relief, etc.

The processes of surface decoration are also very numerous.

Some of the early embossed pieces are spotted with patches of cobalt blue. Upon others the ornaments are scratched in with a point and the lines filled in with powdered zaffre.

FIG. 43. BEAR JUG.—COLL. L. S.

Light blue Stone-ware paste used for applied ornament or for the ground in the same manner as blue jasper.

Decoration with dots of red slip or lines of manganese.

Deep cuttings in the body with a blade, diamond shape, or diagonal lines as upon some German pieces.

14

Shavings of clay strewn on the surface so as to form rough bands alternating with smooth ones, or all over the piece as in the bears (Fig. 43).

Blue Salt-glaze, the whole piece covered with a blue ground under the glaze.

Tin-glaze combined with the Salt-glaze, either for the ground or painted on in opaque decoration.

Enamelling in all sorts of styles.

Fig. 44. Scratched Blue Ware.—Coll. L. S.

Size gilding or varnish painting.

Printing in red or black, etc.

Some of the above processes deserve special attention. The "scratched blue," for instance, enjoyed a successful run (Fig. 44). The ware is always neatly and skilfully potted, but, as a contrast, the decoration is so barbarous, that many would not hesitate to refer it to the remotest infancy of art. After having been finished by the turner, it passed into the hands of women called "flowerers," who with a pointed tool scratched in the wet clay a cursive design of their own imagining, and, with a flock of cotton wool, dusted in the hollow lines powdered zaffre or smalt, that is to say, a sort of glass coloured with cobalt, that for the sake of cheapness the potters used for a long time in preference to the expensive oxide. They never attained to a very high proficiency, nor does any master seem to have ever taken care to supply them with good patterns.

Cobalt and zaffre had been but recently introduced in the Potteries, probably in consequence of the trials of Delft-ware made by *T. Heath*, of Lane Delph, in 1710. Early pieces of Staffordshire pottery do not exhibit a trace of its use, and it is not comprised amongst the metallic oxides that were employed to decorate the Tortoiseshell. Jugs and mugs of scratched blue ware were in great demand for public houses, and unlike other specimens of Salt-glaze, they often bear dates and inscriptions, many of them referring to elections and other public events. The gift of a mug was one form of bribery. One of them, preserved in the British Museum, has: "Sir William a plumper," and was made on the occasion of the Liverpool contest in 1761. Another, in Lady Charlotte Schreiber's collection, is inscribed with four verses in honour of the King of Prussia, 1758. In our own collection a circular pocket flask is dated 1766.

The white Salt-glaze pieces which came out of the mould covered with embossments, and were produced by the hundred, left the casting shop completely finished, and no particular handiwork distinguished one from the other. The scratched blue, on the contrary, had to receive a fancy decoration, which could in each instance be made different; and often, as a matter of course, the workman supplemented his design with inscriptions of names and dates. Thus it happens that, while the white pieces are seldom, if ever, inscribed, the blue ones are generally so, and many examples are dated from 1750 to 1780.

Wedgwood, it is said, began by making this sort of ware during his first partnership with *Harrison*, of Stoke. We can imagine what must have been his dismay when, after he had caused a piece to be thrown and turned with the greatest care and precision, he saw it thus scrawled over by inexperienced hands. Was it from this that during his whole career he decidedly preferred the repeated reproduction of a work modelled under his own eyes by select sculptors, to any painting that could be freely executed upon a plain surface?

We assisted in the unearthing, in some excavations at Hanley, of an enormous heap of diminutive cups without handles, and saucers as thin as egg-shell china, all broken to fragments, and which had been thrown away as imperfect; from this we may see that the makers of scratched blue had great difficulties to contend with.

Earlier than these, and evidently made with the view of competing with the Stone-ware imported from Germany, are the jugs and mugs

FIG. 45. SALT-GLAZE JUG, IMITATION OF GERMAN WARE COLL. L. S.

which bear the medallion, or simply the crowned monogram of George I. and George II. (Fig. 45); they are thinner and whiter than the pieces they strove to emulate; they are likewise incised with deep lines, coloured over with dark blue, and ribbed on the top and bottom. The imitation is by no means a servile one; the body is the same as that used for the ordinary Salt-glaze pieces, and does not resemble the Flemish grey stone-ware, of which many examples, also stamped with the monogram "G. R.," remain for comparison; the decoration is clumsy, being even below the awkward scrawling seen on the English scratched blue, the colour having been only coarsely spread with a rag soaked in liquid blue. Usually these pieces are attributed to Fulham, but we know that a much better imitation of the foreign article was produced there; and fragments dug up in the Staffordshire Potteries warrant our supposing that they were manufactured in that locality.

Jugs, mugs, and jars are frequently met with, and they are all cleverly thrown, turned, and handled. They were, no doubt, commonly made for the use of public-houses, and bear the royal effigy, with the monogram "G. R.," which stood then as a guarantee of their being of the legal capacity. A small jug in the Liverpool Museum, identical in body and shape with the piece represented in Fig. 45, is said to have been made by *J. Malkin*, in 1690; but little reliance can be placed on a family tradition which no other facts corroborate.

About 1750, Salt-glaze, which so far had been decorated with only random touches of blue or brown, was thought fit to receive enamel decoration, with the intention of thereby rivalling the costly china made at Chelsea and Worcester. As the manufacturers of these last-named places chiefly aimed at reproducing the patterns of Eastern Porcelain, so did the first enamellers in Staffordshire, and it is not to be wondered at if painting on Salt-glaze did not keep in the track of originality opened by the first "block cutters."

FIG. 46. ENAMELLED SALT-GLAZE.—COLL. L. S.

Besides, the earliest pieces were not, and could not be, painted by local artists, as no hands had yet been trained to that style of decoration. Two painters, names unknown, came from Holland and settled in Hot Lane, near Burslem. They used to buy white Stone-ware from the potters, and to enamel it in great secrecy, painting it with flowers and figures in a pseudo-Chinese manner (Fig. 46). For a long time the manufacturers were dependent on decorators wholly unconnected with their pot works. Private persons came from Liverpool, Bristol, and Worcester, for the purpose of buying Salt-glaze ware, and decorating it on the spot. This practice was all the easier as only a small muffle was required for enamel painting. The effect was charming, as we can see from the numerous pieces that have come down to us, the brilliancy of the enamels forming a striking contrast with the subdued whitish tint of the ground.

Very soon the number of artists so employed in the Potteries increased considerably, but improvements in the manufactories were not quickly effected in a locality so remote, and where the other industries of the period had as yet hardly penetrated. The potters could not seek any help or derive any hints from any other collateral branch of the trade. In large towns, where stained glass windows were painted, and where goldsmiths covered their work with bright enamels, the earthenware decorators might have been earlier made acquainted with recipes of colours and enamels which would have met their special wants. It was indeed in this way that the first china painters proceeded on the Continent; but such assistance was not available in Staffordshire, so the potters had to wait once more until foreign assistance came to the rescue.

The pieces which may be attributed to the two Dutchmen who had settled at Hot Lane were, as far as enamelling goes, as good patterns as could possibly be procured; they show a skill in the pencilling which may vie with the most costly piece of English china, and their colours may stand the comparison with the brightest enamels. Their decoration, of a would-be Chinese style, clearly recalls the art of the Dutch faïence painters, who, after having studied the eastern porcelain in its general characteristics rather than copy any special design, let their fancy run loose upon subjects of their own imagination, treated somewhat in a Chinese manner. It was no doubt to these two Dutchmen that were due the first productions of this new style of painting, soon imitated all over the district, and applied not only to Salt-glaze but also to cream-coloured earthenware.

Daniel, of Cobridge, was the first local potter who practised enamelling in his factory, and his example was soon followed by others. This was the highest improvement that could be applied to the ware. It perfected and completed its manufacture. It achieved at once a great success, principally because it became in that way a fairly good substitute for the painted china so much in fashion, but which, on account of its exorbitant price, was only to be indulged in by the wealthiest class. Either the embossments were followed by the painter, and relieved with colours, or else patterns were traced across them in a free and off-hand manner. Chinese decorations were

FIG. 47. ENAMELLED SALT-GLAZE.—COLL. L. S.

often imitated; sometimes engravings were copied, or the artist chose to exert his imagination upon figure subjects or pastoral compositions, in costumes of the period. We possess a tea canister painted with garden scenes, each comprising several personages and an elaborate landscape

(Fig. 47); in front is a delicately worked ornament, probably the reproduction of a book plate, surrounding the words "Fine Bohea Tea;" the whole is beautifully executed. A coffee pot, also in our own collection, is painted with flowers in the Chelsea style, probably by some one who had come over from that manufactory. Many are the pieces which have the portrait of the King of Prussia, the favourite hero of the time. On a curious crabstock handle teapot, of which many copies are still in existence, his profile is enamelled in proper colour, while the whole ground is dotted over with small black strokes to represent ermine. We have several specimens of various coloured grounds—red, maroon, blue, and green; small white medallions are reserved, upon which are painted landscapes or bouquets of flowers, somewhat in the Worcester style. By the additional process of size gilding, these pieces are made to look very handsome, and there is little excuse left for their aristocratic models to give themselves airs of superiority. The enamels on all these pieces shine with the brightest hues; the turquoise blue especially would bear comparison with the best soft china colour, and they stand out all the better by the contrast they offer to the dull grey tint of the body. In many cases so much skill and finish have been bestowed on the painting, that we cannot help thinking it would attract much greater admiration if it had only been executed upon a finer material. At any rate, the decoration seldom lacks the style and character so often missing from highly valued examples of English china. For this reason the artist cannot but look with partiality upon the best pieces of enamelled Salt-glaze, and praise their decorative effect.

The traces of half-obliterated gilding remaining on some pieces show that gold was often introduced in the decoration, but the potters did not yet know how to burn it in. We learn from *Wedgwood's* letters, that in 1765 he himself was still busy trying to overcome the difficulty. Leaf gold, secured with size or varnish, was employed, and burnished gold was not practised in the Potteries until some years later, when some workmen brought the process over from the Derby manufactory.

We have said that the use of plaster moulds took away many of the artistic features of the early Salt-glaze. The facility with which casts could be taken from metal or china pieces, led to the reproduction of many admired models, and the ware, which had kept its originality for such a long time, was debased into mere copies. So we find the "bee jug," of Bow, made of white Stoneware, and salt cellars with shells and sea-weeds, similar to those of Plymouth. In Mr. Willett's collection is a group of several figures, imitating white porcelain so perfectly that it might deceive anyone at a first glance. *Wedgwood's* jasper was also imitated. Mr. Shadford Walker, of Liverpool, has two medallions on a blue ground, with applied portraits of *Josiah Wedgwood* and his wife, after the pictures by Stubbs. These medallions at one time were very commonly found in the Potteries. As Delft tiles made at Liverpool or abroad were extensively used for fire-places or decorative purposes, tiles in stamped Salt-glaze were manufactured to compete with them. We possess a set of these which came from *Whieldon's* own house. They were probably made by him, as the same patterns are also found decorated with his usual "tortoiseshell" process. They represent landscapes and animals, and the moulds used were carved after the old fashion.

The perforated porcelain plates and dishes brought over from Dresden gave rise to a new style of dessert services, perforated on the rim, and embossed all over with basket work, and various ornaments; for the modest admirer who could not afford the expense of such costly luxury as foreign china, fruit baskets and plates, cut out with equal delicacy, were manufactured in Salt-glaze ware, and being comparatively cheap, met with a ready sale. They were not copies, but distant reminiscences; and a certain pattern cut in the mould by *Aaron Wood*, and evincing an incontestable originality, is now in every collection. An enormous quantity must have been produced, for even in our days it would not be difficult to bring together entire services of it. In the same manner open-work fruit baskets of a fragile character, made like real wicker work, or with an open design, the intricacy of which dispensed with any addition of painting or gilding, cruet stands, and puzzle jugs were made. We have a charming sweet box, formed of a double shell; the outer one, thin as an ordinary sheet of cardboard, is perforated with numerous holes which show the inner box in the same way as certain Chinese puzzles. The most delicate perforations were practised upon thinly turned pieces with steel tools, cutting out the hole at one blow in the required shape, so, by "punching" as it was called, the top of a jug or the rim of a plate could, with very little trouble, be made to look marvellously worked.

The manufacture of Salt-glaze was not confined to Staffordshire. At Jackfield it was made early in the eighteenth century, although, probably, only in imitation of the ware made in the adjoining county, and there, towards 1763, *Simpson* manufactured pipe-clay ware glazed with salt for the American market.

At Leeds, white and enamelled Salt-glaze preceded the manufacture of cream-coloured earthenware. The Rev. T. Stanniforth possesses a white jug painted with enamels, and inscribed with the name of the town.

At Liverpool, quantities of "wasters" have been found on the site of *Shaw's* manufactory, and many stamped pieces bear the liver, the bird which is the crest of the town. The rare printed plates may also have been made there.

At Swansea, according to Chaffers, a very thin Salt-glaze ware, roughly but effectively decorated with bright enamels, was made about 1780, and some of the specimens are marked "Cambrian Pottery." It was probably made at many other places, of which no records remain. It is said that a small manufactory lingered at Burslem until 1823.

In our time the wafer-like white stone-ware glazed with salt has gone the way of the heavy Delft; they both had their day, and then ceased to be.

More, perhaps, than any other English ware, the Salt-glaze excites the interest we feel for any artistic production which speaks to us of by-gone times, obsolete taste, and vanished customs; in short it does look *old;* older, indeed, than many pieces that can boast of a much more ancient pedigree. Independently of their proper merits, an old painting darkened and mellowed by age, an oxidized bronze, a weather-beaten building, or a time-worn statue, possesses an attractive charm that age alone has imparted. A feeling of the same sort, a mingled sensation of liking and curiosity, has from the first attracted us towards the strange-looking specimens of early Salt-glaze ware. Their soft creamy tint recalls that of old ivory, and the glossy surfaces of both offer resemblances; the designs, simple and "naïf" as they are, may be compared for their conventionality to those which adorn the pages of Gothic MSS. If we add to this, that most of these embossed and wafer-like pieces have come out from the firing twisted and crooked, and so are very different from anything else the eye generally rests upon, we shall see at once how difficult it would be, by a mere process of comparison with other artistic objects, to ascribe any definite age to them. One can easily understand how "Elizabethan ware" was thought to be at first a suitable name, when little or nothing was known of the Staffordshire Potteries, and of the potters who, for more than a century, had spread their productions all over England.

Few things are left for the amateur of the future; even for him of the present day who cannot command an unlimited supply of money, collecting begins to be a hopeless pursuit; all has been gathered, classified, and priced, all excepting the works of the old English Potter; many are still about, to be picked up at a small price for the gratification of the few who, like ourselves, delight in studying and admiring these primitive productions. It is not too late to begin to form collections, and we hope that one day we shall see the Early English earthenware valued and appreciated as it deserves to be.

CHAPTER VII.

EARTHENWARE.

CREAM-COLOUR, AGATE WARE, TORTOISESHELL, ETC.

ANTIQUITY OF EARTHENWARE—ITS REVIVAL BY ENGLISH POTTERS.—IMPROVEMENTS IN EARTHENWARE FOLLOWING ON THE RESEARCHES FOR A WHITE BODY.—INCREASE IN THE TRADE OF THE POTTERIES TOWARDS THE BEGINNING OF THE EIGHTEENTH CENTURY.—INTRODUCTION OF FLINT AND CREAM-COLOUR WARE.—TORTOISESHELL AND COLOURS UNDER GLAZE.—PATENTS.—AGATE WARE.—THOMAS ASTBURY.—RALPH SHAW.—JOHN MITCHELL.—THOMAS AND JOHN WEDGWOOD.—THOMAS WHIELDON.—SHAPES AND MODELS.—IMITATIONS AND PIRACIES.—INTRODUCTION INTO THE POTTERIES OF BLUE PAINTING ON EARTHENWARE.—ENAMELLING. — FOREIGN CHINA PAINTERS WORKING IN ENGLAND. — PLASTER MOULDS AND THEIR EFFECT. — LAST IMPROVEMENTS IN CREAM-COLOUR.

EARTHENWARE.

THE history of the best English earthenware glazed with lead is so intimately linked with the records of the manufacture of common pottery in the earliest times, the one being so necessarily the outgrowth of the other, that it is difficult to fix the date when the fabric entered on the course of improvements by which it gradually came to assert itself as the cheapest, the neatest, and the most suitable ware that could be contrived to supply our ordinary wants, and ultimately superseded all the more complicated processes which previously had had their turn of fashion and success. A little more care in the potting and in the way of applying the glaze, and the vessels of the middle ages might have rivalled most of the cream-colour pieces made in the eighteenth century. The common marl of the country, mixed with pipe-clay and a little sand, constituted a plastic body which could be worked easily and quickly, and also fired safely; as to glazing, the lead ore or "galena" demanded but little preparation, and the colours were all obtained with the oxides of such well-known metals as were in after times thought sufficient for the production of a much higher class of ware; so the groundwork the potter had to improve upon was simple and sound. With these commonplace materials, marvels of the fictile art had occasionally been accomplished, masterpieces, as remarkable for the beauty and purity of their shapes as the harmony of their colours. Nevertheless, earthenware potting remained stationary for a long time, as we have seen, and there was no demand for it. The lower classes were satisfied with the wooden utensils or coarse clay pans that answered their daily requirements; and for show, even well-to-do people preferred to anything else the tin dishes that most resembled the silver plate which adorned the dresser of the titled and the wealthy. The requisites of the dinner table in Staffordshire are so described in the "Potter's Art," a poem privately published at Burslem in 1828, by J. Ward, the author of the "History of Stoke-upon-Trent:"

"The housewife—prim in days we knew ourselves—
Display'd her polish'd *pewter* on her shelves,
Reserved to honor most the annual feast,
When ev'ry kinsman prov'd a welcome guest;
No *earthen* plates or dishes then were known,
Save at the humble board as coarse as stone;
And there the trencher commonly was seen
With its attendant ample platter *treen* (wooden)."

On the Continent the first trials for a refined earthenware were master strokes, and should have led to an important manufacture, yet these attempts do not seem to have been followed up. What could excel, for instance, the style and cleverness of workmanship of the faïence d'Oiron, precious gems formed of the commonest clay? From such a beginning what marvels might not have been expected; but nothing came of it, they remained mere trials, only made to gratify the fancy of a highly-gifted noblewoman, endowed with a keen sense of beauty and a craving for perfection. As soon as the inspiring spirit ceased to direct the efforts of her assistants, their art declined and passed away altogether. In Bauvaisie, at about the same period, the country people were for a time not short of ornamental and artistic pottery; the earthenware potters of Lachapelle des Pots were modelling all sorts of quaint pieces, curiously contrived in shape, and elaborately embossed; nevertheless, their work differed completely from the ware made at Oiron. This latter owes its chief beauty to grace of form, and to the delicate effect obtained by the pure cream-colour ground being minutely damascened with coloured clays. In the case of the ware of Lachapelle des Pots, on the other hand, the ground is all covered with rich glazes, exhausting the gamut of the powerful harmonies that can be obtained with metallic oxides. The unknown potters of Bauvaisie were the forerunners of *Palissy*, who shortly afterwards showed what more could be still achieved by means of the ordinary clay stained with coloured glazes; his indomitable energy and his refined taste raised his art to so high a level, that it became a hopeless task for his successors to attempt to maintain the heavy inheritance which *Palissy* bequeathed to them. The advent of the opaque glaze faïence, which had the advantage of being of a pure and glossy white, and showing brighter colours, threw the works of all these great potters into the shade; their teachings were forgotten, and earthenware ran once more the risk of being relegated to the limbo of materials unworthy of receiving any artistic treatment.

Upon the old English potters devolved the honour of reviving the obsolete manufacture, and thus they became unconsciously the true successors of *Helene of Hangest* and *Palissy;* but where the great artists had only found scope for displaying their unapproachable individuality, the plodding, ingenious, and practical potters of England, working as a body, succeeded in creating, by gradual transformations, a ware so superior to all others, that it affected the conditions of the potting trade in general, and all Europe was influenced and benefited by the discovery.

As far back as we can trace the dawn of the first improvements, we see that along with the red or brown clay, the greyish marl continued to be used in its native state. Both were glazed with "galena" or lead ore, by the primitive process of dusting it over the pieces through a bag of coarse cloth. Light-coloured ware was therefore made concurrently with all other kinds, but no preference seems to have been given to it, at first, over the dark or black vessels that were commonly used; and yet its dull yellowish tint was capable of being vividly coloured, and was better adapted to show the modelling of the surface. Little heed was taken of those qualities. It was chiefly employed as a coating for darker clays, for slip painting, or for applied ornamentation; few, if any, pieces were made of plain yellow clay, unless something exceptional was intended; in short, there was nothing to indicate the important part it was destined to play in the ceramics of the future. When researches for a white ware, glazed with salt, were being actively prosecuted in the pot works of Staffordshire, many combinations of clay had to be experimented upon, and the common earthenware was materially advanced by the experience acquired through the trials made with a view to obtain quite a different body. The production of white Stone-ware required a good deal more care and delicacy than had hitherto been bestowed upon ordinary potting, and yellow clay glazed with lead followed in the track of the newly-invented and more refined ware. Both being manufactured at the same place and by the same men, they kept abreast in the course of successive improvements; the same mould was used whether the piece was to be made of white Stone-ware and fired at a high temperature in the Salt-glaze oven, or of common clay, to be coloured, glazed with lead, and submitted to a lower degree of heat; in one case, to commend itself by the neatness of shape and details; in the other, made attractive by its deep harmony of colours profusely flowing over the surface. It is as though we found there again the old contention of drawing and colour striving for precedence. We may be allowed to remark here that richness of hue seems to have been the natural bent of English taste. In its early and most genuine productions it affects a decided tendency towards bright and showy colours. It is only when the fact is denounced by some cold-blooded reformer that people seem to rush unanimously to the opposite extreme, discarding what they best liked. Ashamed one day of their natural feelings of admiration, they allow themselves to be talked into accepting anything that may be palmed off upon them as models, and so the conventionality and stiffness of a so-called high style may be substituted for the charms of a genuine and unsophisticated art. In Ceramics, as in painting, the English artist begins by showing himself a true colourist, and yet the lively and harmonious pottery of the commencement had to make room for the dull and formal cream-colour and monochrome earthenware which prevailed at the end of the eighteenth century. We may well ask ourselves what had become of the promise contained in the powerful productions of the tortoiseshell period; misplaced self-criticism and a too severe repression of innate propensities, in more instances than this, waylaid English art and turned it from its natural channel.

During the whole course of the seventeenth century, many different processes were in embryo amongst the potters of Staffordshire, but production continued to be limited, and little progress was noticeable in the extension of their trade; when suddenly, towards the beginning of the following century, a rage for improvement sets in, and within a few years pervades the whole district. Everyone is at work bringing his small stone to the monument. Some are sedulously engaged mixing and trying all clays and minerals that can be procured at home; others, more enterprising, take the unwonted step of travelling long distances in quest of fresh materials and suggestive models. With an astounding rapidity changes follow upon changes, pottery is applied to all sorts of fresh uses, ovens are built all over the district, and a flourishing industry is established for exportation as well as for home trade. Notwithstanding the rapid increase of population in the surrounding country, farmers find themselves short of hands; crops can hardly be gathered in, and tradesmen in towns cannot any longer obtain apprentices. All men and women go to the pot works, where there is never a sufficient supply of labour, and where wages soon grow to be uncommonly high for skilful workmen.

The numerous patents granted at that time in connection with earthenware are a sign of the prevalent excitement and the general desire for novelties. We shall give further on a few of their specifications, though little can be made of their obscure phraseology. They have only a secondary interest for us, when we remember that such important discoveries as caused a revolution in the trade were never patented at all. Up to that time, as we have seen, the lightest ware was of a dull, smoky tint, still further darkened by the thick coating of sulphuret of lead, either dusted over the piece or unevenly applied with a hair pencil. The most interesting and effectual innovations bore upon the two principal desiderata of the potters of the day, namely, obtaining a perfectly white body, which, being easily formed into shape, should not crack in the firing, and a colourless fluid glaze. These two wants were supplied, by *Astbury's* introduction of flint bodies in 1720, and, at an interval of thirty years, by *E. Booth's* method of dipping the ware into an improved glaze kept in suspension in water.

As soon as *Astbury* had fixed the exact proportion of flint that was to enter into its composition, the earthenware body may be said to have been invented and settled. We shall not question the veracity of the oft-told tale, relating how he was delayed in one of his journeys to London, to have the injured eye of his horse attended to by a farrier, who, taking a black flint stone, calcined it in the fire, then crushing it into a fine powder, blew the dust into the horse's eye; in short, how it happened that the potter, being struck with the whiteness of the material, caused a wagon load of flint stones to be brought to Shelton, where he successfully combined the calcined powder with his ordinary clays.

The story, which, by-the-bye, is by some attributed to a Mr. Heath, of Shelton, may be true, or may rank amongst other doubtful anecdotes. Notwithstanding the knowledge we possess of pounded flint having been employed by *Dwight* in the composition of some of his bodies, and the probability that *Dwight* was not the first to use it, since he does not set up any claims to the discovery, it remains an undisputed fact that to *Astbury* alone was due the credit, if not of having found out quite a new material, at all events of having determined in what proportions it was to be added to the compound body which no one had made before him, and which remained for ever after, in spite of small modifications, about the same as he had left it, under whatever name his "cream colour" may have been subsequently disguised.

At first the attention of inventors was chiefly directed towards technicalities, perfecting clays and glazes, and improving their manipulation; all had to be found out; and before they thought of endowing the ware with artistic qualities, they strove to secure a safe ground to work upon. This is the reason why we may now admire unreservedly their most unpretentious early pieces, the fruit of these first experiments and researches, observing how the clays are well ground and levigated; what perfection is at once reached in the turning and moulding of a simple teapot; how the lid fits well each piece; how sharp are the lines, and true the shape. A good make is the main consideration, and, even for decoration, design comes only second to the process employed.

The strenuous efforts of the Staffordshire potters had at last succeeded in obtaining a white ware, for which there was a great demand; the flint bodies, either cream-colour glazed with lead or Salt-glazed stone-ware, steadily acquired more whiteness by successive improvements; but at the same time the potters made a labour of love of experimenting upon their coloured clays and glazes, the continuation of the works of their fathers, an inheritance they jealously kept and enlarged day by day. There was no sign of their giving up making the dry red-ware, finely stamped with seals, or the highly glazed pieces of dark yellow or bright red clay relieved with coloured applications. While many preferred the fanciful and ever-varied pieces brilliant with the harmonious hues of divers coloured glazes, others continued to show their partiality for the shining black tea-ware, which made such a contrast with the spotless table-cloth. There has, indeed, always been in England a decided liking for black ware; and although it was manufactured in many places on the Continent, nowhere does it seem to have so well suited the public taste as in this country. From the first trials made by the *Elers* in the dry bodies, and the black glazed Tygs of Staffordshire, the ware was constantly made and improved upon, until it became the black basalt of *Josiah Wedgwood;* nay, since his time the manufacture has never been discontinued.

Under the name of "clouded" or "mottled,"

earthenware, coloured with metallic oxides, had been for a long time before produced; this doubtless led to the imitation of tortoiseshell, so effectively carried out by means of manganese spotted with a sponge over the dry clay; simple

FIG. 48. TORTOISESHELL COFFEE POT.—COLL. L. S.

as this process was, the aptitude of certain workmen realised with it some astonishing results obtained by the well-contrasted shades of the opaque and the transparent parts (Fig. 48). The success was immense, and the name of "tortoiseshell," which had been given to that ware, was so readily recognized by the public, that the same name extended to everything that was mottled under glaze with varied colours; we shall also keep to the same word with regard to pieces of this class whenever we may have to refer to them. Copper green, antimony, ochre yellow, manganese, and sometimes a touch of zaffre, were the only oxides used, and the colours blended in a remarkable manner when melting under a thick and smooth glaze; this was partly owing to their being fired in the same oven alternately with Salt-glaze, the brickwork and saggers being so much soaked with melted salt, that the vapours of soda pervaded all the atmosphere during the firing, acting upon the colours as a flowing agent. This method may probably account for Shaw having mistaken the old cream-colour for white stone-ware, and for his speaking of it as having been indiscriminately glazed with salt or with lead ore.

In 1724, *Robert Redrich* and *Thomas Jones* took out a patent for "staining, veining, spotting, clouding, damascening, or otherwise imitating the various kinds of marble, porphyry, and other rich stones, tortoiseshell, etc., on wood, stone, or earthenware." As we can see from this specification that the process could be applied to wood or stone as well as earthenware, it was necessarily a surface one, and may be regarded as a derivation from that used for marbling papers; with regard to its application to pottery it offered little novelty, for the imitation of tortoiseshell as well as the combed ware had been practised a long time before.

But this leads us to speak of the "*Agate-ware*" which *Dr. Thomas Wedgwood*, son of *Thomas Wedgwood*, of the Overhouse Works, at Burslem, is said to have made in great perfection. On the site of his manufactory, when digging the foundations of a new market, many fragments were disinterred. Agate-ware was a complicated process; the marbling, instead of being produced on the surface, went through the body. It was thus practised:—Thin laminæ of yellow and red clay were laid alternately upon each other until they formed a thick mass; from that mass thin slices were transversely cut with a wire, making thin bats which showed the veining produced by the superimposed layers of clays; these slices were then used to press the piece, the neatest side being placed against the mould. In the case of a square mould being used, as shown in Fig. 49, the veining lost nothing of its neatness, but, as a rule, the bat required careful handling, as a pressure sideways in the wedging in, or a too rough pressing in the mould destroyed the fineness in the marbling. Nothing more delicate could be formed from clay, especially when they were finished and polished on the lathe, and either glazed in their natural colours, red and yellow, or different shades of brown and red, or else stained with a blue glaze, which imparted to the mixture the fine greyish hue of agate. Pieces of a small size alone, such as tea ware, pickle trays, sauce boats, and snuff boxes, were made of these mixed bodies. Seldom do they show any embossment; round pieces got

FIG. 49. AGATE-WARE.—COLL. L. S.

a better surface by turning. A purse-shaped teapot, of which several replicas are known, may be considered as an exception; its shape is ribbed in imitation of the shell teapots then commonly made in Salt-glaze, but without any of their intricate details; a flat slice of marbled clay could not have been forced into narrow cavities without losing its fine veining through the requisite manipulation, consequently the original shape has been rounded, softened, and smoothed, to facilitate the pressing. It is worth noticing that these Agate-ware pieces are certainly anterior in date to the supposed introduction of the process of pressing in the Staffordshire Potteries. We may hazard the supposition that casting and throwing were generally preferred, and that pressing was confined to a limited use long before it became commonly employed at the time fixed by tradition.

The knife hafts so extensively manufactured by *Dr. Thomas Wedgwood* and *Whieldon* for the cutlers of Sheffield are precisely similar in body and glaze to this specimen, and we may refer it to one of these two potters, probably the latter, considering its perfection. The innovation introduced in the making of Agate-ware, by which it differs from the mixed clays employed a very long time before, is the transverse cutting through the mass with a wire, which gave a fineness and continuity to the lines of the marbling unobtainable by the ordinary mode of blending the clays, and the pressing in a mould instead of throwing on the wheel, by which the veining was disturbed. At Fulham, *Dwight* produced a sort of Agate-ware, with grey and white Stone-ware; and many common pieces of the same period are streaked with light and dark clays. Early, in Staffordshire, different coloured clays were also blended together in a rough way, so as to imitate marble; in that manner large slabs were made, some destined to be inserted in the walls of houses, recording the name of the owner and the year of construction; others, with inscriptions scratched in, or laid on with slip, were set up over graves; some of these are still to be seen in the churchyards of the Potteries.

Another patent was granted in 1729 to *Samuel Bell* for a new method of making a red marble Stone-ware to imitate ruby. Of this we are not able to give any account, unless it referred to a variety of bright red and yellow Agate-ware, a specimen of which is in our collection, and is the only one of the sort we ever came across.

Agate-ware, that is to say, a marbling going through the whole substance, was never made to the same extent as marbling on the surface. On the latter *Josiah Wedgwood* made some of his favourite experiments, and he imitated very successfully and effectively all sorts of Agates and hard stones by running, mixing, and spotting various coloured slips upon the cream colour. Nearly all the potters of his day followed his lead, and produced many surface mixtures which still went by the name of Agate, although the objects on which it was used would be more properly described by the name of "marbled" ware.

Reverting to the history of the improvements

brought about in the making of earthenware and cream-colour, we think we could not do better than recall the names of some of the most ingenious potters of Staffordshire, and mention the share which each had in the collective movement. Two names stand out conspicuously in the numerous lists: *Astbury*, who by the introduction of flint may rightly claim to have created a new ware; and *Whieldon*, who, a few years later, brought it to so high a degree of perfection, by the care he bestowed upon its manufacture, and the taste he displayed in the selection of his models, that *Josiah Wedgwood* found little to improve in the cream-colour of his day, when he transformed it into his celebrated "Queen's ware."

Had *Astbury* ever thought, like *Palissy*, of writing his "memoirs," we should have had a book which would not have yielded in romantic interest even to the autobiography of the French potter. The business of a pot-maker was then a very precarious one. No man who was ambitious of making a fortune would have embraced that trade; the highest position a workman could hope to reach was that of owner of a single oven, turning out weekly a limited quantity of goods to be sold for a paltry profit to the cratemen, or at the neighbouring fair. *John Astbury*, although very young, was established in a small way like his fellow-workers, and he seems to have been alive to the unsatisfactory state of the manufacture of his time; so, when the *Elers* had settled near Burslem, he could not help contrasting their delicate productions with the rough and common pottery which had up to that time been made around him. Leaving his unattractive business, he made up his mind to worm out their secrets, and thus enlarge his scanty and insufficient knowledge. What hardship he had to go through, in order to get admittance into the premises without exciting suspicion, has been often related. For two years, it is said, he feigned idiocy in its most abject state, until at last, considering that he had acquired all that could be mastered from his employers' processes, he threw off the disguise and set to work earnestly on his own account in quite a new style, with all sorts of fresh methods. The morals of the time admitted to a certain extent of such questionable proceedings, especially when dealing with hated foreigners. In our day such conduct would perhaps be differently regarded, and yet there is more than one redeeming point in the case of *Astbury*. We must acknowledge that he did not confine himself to reproducing exactly the same things he had seen made by the *Elers*. He originated more than one style of his own by mixing up the new notions with the old ones. He established a compromise between the common pieces of dark clay glazed with galena, and the refined and highly finished ware that the Dutchmen had called red porcelain. The dense and dry body of his masters became in his hands a red glazed ware. The expensive piece was altered into a nearly similar one, which, by its cheapness, met the wants of the million. New articles, such as tea and coffee ware, dessert plates, and similar pieces, which had been only exceptionally made before his time, were manufactured by him in large quantities. New clays and fresh materials were unceasingly experimented upon, until a new body was at last established. It is most interesting to follow the efforts of the early potter, who, unable to diversify his productions by painting or hand decoration, had to contrive all sorts of combinations of clays, to give them a little variety. Limited as the means were, very varied in effect do we find the examples that belong to the same period; they present every possible arrangement of buff, dark yellow, red, brown, and white, being sometimes finished off with a few touches of under-glaze colours. Thus *Astbury* tried the white clay employed by the pipe-makers; but before being able to produce a good ware from it, he only used it at first for the small ornamentation stamped on the dark ground, and soon after as a wash inside the vessels, which, though made of red clay in the bulk, were on the inside coated with a lining of light yellow. But what entitles him to the gratitude of his contemporaries and successors is the fact that he, who had taken so much pains to get at the secrets of the Dutch potters, does not appear to have made a mystery of all that it cost him so much to acquire. He worked, after all, for the public at large. Owing to his sole exertions the whole district made rapid progress, and all the craft was benefited whenever he achieved some fresh discovery. Modest and painstaking he surely was, to judge from the manner in which he conducted his pot work. It is even said that he did not like to give free play to his inventive genius for fear of upsetting the uses and customs of his fellow-potters, and thereby come to be looked upon as a revolutionary character. There is no doubt, however, about his having been an enterprising man of business. He was one of the first who travelled to increase his business connection; and at a time when, on account of the bad state of the roads, travelling was attempted by but few, he used to make regular and periodical journeys to London and the large towns of the Midlands, whither he carried himself the ingenious patterns he had innovated for that purpose during the course of the year.

Contrary to the practice on the Continent, where each manufacturer limited himself to a speciality, the English potter had always a great variety of bodies and glazes to work with at one and the same time. Along the Rhine is found the Grès Stone-ware, and in Holland the white faïence with a stanniferous glaze; each factory of Italy kept to a special style of decoration, almost sufficient for identification, and a great difference distinguishes one French ware from another. If we take such potters as *Astbury, Whieldon,* and their contemporaries, we find that within their small premises all sorts of ware were concurrently manufactured—red or black body, either dry or glazed; white Stone-ware glazed with salt; cream-colour, glazed with lead, plain, and coloured with tortoiseshell enamels; even, in a few instances, Delft-ware with blue painting.

We have seen that towards 1720 *Astbury* made his name famous by the introduction of pounded flint into common earthenware; it is plain that he would not or could not keep the secret of the discovery to himself, but, on the contrary, that he soon allowed it to spread all over the Potteries, and this is clearly shown by the patent *Benson* took out, in 1726, for a new method of grinding flint-stone; heretofore, it is said, iron mortars had been used for that purpose, and the dust produced by the pounding was most injurious to the health of the workmen. *Benson* conceived the idea of grinding it under water. *Astbury* was not long in realising the importance of the invention, and flint was ground in that way for the first time in a mill erected at his own expense at a place called the Ivy House, near Hanley. He died at Shelton, in 1743, being then 65 years of age, a rich and highly-considered man, at the same place where he had started as a potter in such humble circumstances. The site of his factory, which stood near the church, was excavated a few years ago, and many fragments were found by which the identification of his productions was greatly facilitated. He left three sons; one of them, *Thomas Astbury*, commenced business at Lane Delph in 1725; he still further improved upon the new ware invented by his father, and it was he who gave it the name of "cream-colour."

Of *Twyford*, who also played the part of an idiot to penetrate into the *Elers'* secrets, little is known; by some he is said to have worked conjointly with *Astbury*, by others to have had a factory of his own in the same town, the site of which belonged to *Thomas Fenton*, the brother of the poet. A small jug of brown ware decorated with slip and inscribed with that name, still in the hands of the family, is the only authenticated piece of *Twyford's* make that we have been so far able to discover.

Of *Dr. Thomas Wedgwood*, and of his making a much improved ware as early as 1731, we have already spoken; we must add that he was considered the best potter of the district. The fragments dug out on the site of his works at Burslem testify to the perfection of his buff and white salt-glaze, his dry red body, and his agate ware. Charming little teapots and jugs of dark yellow clay, relieved with applications of white designs, stamped on in the style of the *Elers*, and touched up with flowing colours, seem to have been his favourite speciality

Ralph Shaw, of Burslem, had his short days of celebrity; in 1733 he patented a so-called invention for making a chocolate ware coated with white, the upper coat being scratched in with lines and flowers; of this we have already spoken in the previous chapter. The specification of his patent was so worded that *Shaw* thought for a time it would give him the right of prosecuting most of the potters of the district for infringements. A test case created great excitement when it came on for trial at Stafford; but he was not able to substantiate his claims to any exclusive rights, the process he revindicated as his own having been used long before by *Astbury*, and he was nonsuited. In his disappointment and humiliation he left the country, and emigrated to France with his family; there he settled and carried on his trade. It would be interesting to investigate whether it is to him that is due the first manufacture of the French "Terre de pipe," and other imitations of English ware. We know that a company of Englishmen established a factory at Montereau in 1775,—a certain *Shaw* was one of them; but whether it was *Ralph Shaw*, or another of the same name, we have had, so far, no means of ascertaining. To his name is attached a really valuable and practical improvement, the introduction of the "slip kiln." Previously the diluted clay had to be evaporated in the open air in large tanks called "sun pans." Not only was the evaporation slowly effected, but the slip was liable to be spoiled with dust. *Shaw* kept it under cover in long troughs, under which ran a row of flues heated from a stove outside; this expeditious process was so well appreciated that it was at once adopted at all the factories. He also found a way of firing a larger quantity of ware in his ovens, by placing the pieces inside each other, ingeniously parting and propping them by bits of stone-ware, so that they could not stick together, an invention which led to the stilts and cockspurs of to-day. But notwithstanding the ameliorations that he introduced in the trade, by which his contemporaries were benefited, it is to be regretted that his contentious spirit may have checked for a time the course of improvements pursued by other potters, and that at last it obliged him to leave the country where he might otherwise have attained to wealth and consideration. Part of his family returned to Burslem in 1750, but he himself remained abroad, and nothing is known as to the date or place of his death.

In 1736, *John Mitchell* was making the same description of ware, and was one of those prosecuted by *Shaw* for infringement of his patent. Great attention was beginning to be paid at that time to the beauty of shapes and models, so *Mitchell* secured, at a comparatively high price, the services of *Aaron Wood*, the best block-cutter of the time, in order that he might be able to compete with *Dr. Thomas Wedgwood*, then at the head of the trade.

In 1740, *Thomas and John Wedgwood*, one a skilful fireman and the other a lead-glaze potter, established themselves at Burslem. The first few years of their partnership are said to have brought them a succession of losses and disappointments. This caused them to make a series of protracted experiments, with the especial view of ascertaining the causes of the many accidents which stood in the way of perfect production, and, particularly, the liability of some clays to crack more than others. They succeeded in fixing a definite scale of their respective qualities, and arranged them according to their order of merit, under the name of "cracking clays;" they also proved that some of the waters, then indiscriminately used, were unfit for potting purposes, and that many accidents were attributable to carelessness on this point. All these studies and many more were very beneficial to the trade in general; and consequently, when their struggles were over, and all their difficulties had been surmounted, owing to the exertions of these two potters, the craft again advanced another step forward. Systematic rules were henceforth adhered to, by which risks were lessened, and, as a matter of course, profits largely increased. Their cream-colour was considered excellent, and they exported it to foreign parts in hitherto unprecedented quantities.

Thomas Whieldon commenced business prior to 1740 at Fenton Low, in a small thatched pot works which was destined gradually to expand into one of the most important manufactories of the time. His business was at first of a very modest sort. Carrying his samples in a bundle strapped to his back, he used to walk from one town to another canvassing for orders. He made first small fancy articles for hardware men, snuff-boxes that were mounted in metal in Birmingham, and Agate-ware knife-hafts for the Sheffield cutlers. Amongst his earliest productions may also be mentioned the quaint little figures, clumsily made up of separate parts of brown and yellow clay, some of which are pressed in moulds, while the others are made by hand. They are but one degree removed from the figures painted on the slip dishes; nevertheless, such a bit of old pitcher may please us by its unpretentious oddity, and we cannot think of lamenting the absence of classical learning when it makes up in "naïveté" for what it lacks in correctness. Thus we still find sets of huntsmen, musicians, soldiers, workmen of the different trades, and also a very characteristic little horseman, the figure being of cream-colour, richly enlivened with green, yellow, and brown, and the horse of black clay, with white trappings. Children's toys, and small mantel-piece ornaments were also made at the same time. To these he soon added the manufacture of table and tea-ware, mostly tortoiseshell, for which he acquired such a reputation, that all the numerous specimens of his style, although made by a crowd of imitators, have since been known under the name of *Whieldon* ware.

As his connection increased, he built, in 1749, large additions to his works. Mr. L. Jewitt (*Life of Josiah Wedgwood*) gives some interesting extracts from his account books, and several invoices, which show us the sort of ware *Whieldon* commonly made. While other potters were pursuing a course which would have ruined the trade, by underselling each other, and turning out a ware so coarse and clumsy that, notwithstanding its cheapness, it was on the eve of being abandoned by the public, *Whieldon* alone resisted this backward movement. Besides continuing the best traditions of his predecessors, and using the same processes in a perfected way, he brought out many ingenious novelties both in shapes and materials. He was assisted by the best model makers, and with great discrimination he selected his apprentices from amongst the most intelligent youths of the district. They profited so much by his tuition that nearly all of them were eminently successful in after life. *Josiah Spode*, *Robert Garner*, *J. Barker*, and *W. Greatbach* all made a name for themselves in the Potteries. *Josiah Wedgwood* was then twenty-four years of age. He had just terminated his first partnership with *Harrison*, of Stoke, and it is to the credit of *Whieldon* that the latter was able to discern and appreciate the abilities of the young potter, and that he secured him as a partner for five years.

It would be very interesting to discover the share he had in the production of *Whieldon's* most refined pieces. *Wedgwood* was already expert in all the branches of the trade, including throwing, modelling, and the compositions of bodies and glazes. He spent much of his time in the first years of their partnership in making trials and preparing blocks and moulds; and it is not improbable that some of those delicate pickle trays, scalloped plates, perforated tea-pots of tortoiseshell or Agate-ware, now so highly prized, are the work of his own hands. More will no doubt be known to us in some future time about his doings at *Whieldon's;* documents of that period are not wanting, and many fresh ones may one day turn up and throw more light on the subject. We know already that it was he who compounded the bright green glaze so much admired, that by itself alone it caused the success of more than one pattern, all designed to show it off to advantage. The cauliflower, pine-apple, and melon ware derived their charming effect from the green glaze contrasting with the cream-colour. It was employed in various ways; while embossed pieces were mottled with green and yellow, others were covered all over with the green ground. Meanwhile the earthenware had in their hands become so white and pure, that the partners were proud of showing its quality, and frequently abstained from hiding its creamy tint under the then fashionable coloured glazes. They seem to have often preferred making another kind of ware, more quiet in colouration, in which the plain clay was reserved for the ground, while parts only of the reliefs were slightly touched up with a dash of brown, yellow, or green; sometimes a faint cloud of grey was thrown over the handles and spouts. These latter specimens are perhaps the most charming of all, and mark the approaching end of the under-glaze decoration, to which plain earthenware was soon to be preferred.

In the first edition of this work we engraved a

cream-colour jug, which, by a piece of rare good fortune, we have been able to identify as *Whieldon's* own manufacture. The pedigree is a very humble one, but the piece has its credentials. It was made in 1757 for one Ralph Hammersley, who was, we are sorry to say, not a man of great mark, but merely *Whieldon's* milkman! Anything better made than this jug cannot be imagined; it is as thin and true as if it were made of metal, and the raised decoration, all applied by hand, is most artistically arranged. The flowers are tinted with grey, yellow, and green glazes; the monogram and date are painted with red clay, a combination of processes not uncommonly seen on the works of this potter. The method of applying or "sprigging" the reliefs pressed in separate moulds of highly-fired clay is one of the great characteristics of English pottery. It continued to be practised after the plaster moulds had come into use, and *Wedgwood* adhered to it for his Jasper ware; in no other way could he have obtained the unrivalled sharpness of his raised figures and ornamentation.

After a few years of association, tradition, which represents *Whieldon* as a very prudent and cautious man, says that he was not sorry to part from his young partner, of whose daring and enterprising spirit he was rather afraid. Not wishing to embark in any other new-fangled enterprises, but being satisfied with making money, as he had always done, by pursuing quietly the unexhausted vein of his former success, he preferred breaking the partnership, some say even before the term of the agreement had expired. We can hardly credit this statement when we see with what untiring energy *Whieldon* had so far endeavoured to advance his art, and steadily kept at the head of his contemporaries. By him the foreign trade was largely increased, and from his time Staffordshire ware was sent all over the world. Many of his pieces are still found in distant parts. Our friend, Dr. I. Lyons, of Hartford, U.S., has been able to form a collection of tortoiseshell, cauliflower, and other varieties of the time, with specimens picked up in the cottages of Connecticut. Near the place where once stood his thatched pot works, *Whieldon* built for himself a large and elegant house, which is still standing, and where he died in 1798, at a very advanced age.

No sooner had the manipulative and other processes reached the point at which it was difficult, if not impossible, to further improve upon them, than the potter turned his attention to a selection of the models best calculated to bring out all their qualities. The tortoiseshell-ware, with its variety of colours, lent itself to all sorts of combinations, and a special treatment was required for the modelling of the pieces intended to be so decorated. The old potter was either his own modeller, or at least employed none but those who had been brought up in the trade, first as common workmen, then, following a special aptitude, had subsequently drifted into that branch of the art. None was better qualified than the practical man to contrive a design adapted to the means at his disposal. He cared little for imitating the works of other people or other countries, but consulting only his own taste, and profiting by the efforts of his fellow-workers, his style was rational and genuine, being, above all, appropriate to the ways and means by which the work was to be produced.

It was then that the modeller came to the front; the best makers endeavoured to secure at any cost the exclusive assistance of those who promised to become the most ingenious artists. A decided tendency towards fancy shapes, and the picturesque in ornamentation, began to show itself even in the most ordinary pieces. A tea-pot assumed the look of an attractive and dainty little toy, and we hear of the gallants of London offering to their lady-loves pretty tea-pots of Staffordshire ware. The hackneyed ornaments, which had been handed down from father to son, were discarded by the rising generation, and new ideas, as well as new men, kept apace in the march of progress. Leaves and fruits were the inexhaustible stock from which the artist drew at first most of his inspirations. A pickle tray was formed with a common leaf (Fig. 50), delicately marked with all its veining, and glazed with its natural colour, and in the centre a few buds and flowers were symmetrically disposed for the purpose of securing a variety of tints. A fruit—the pine-apple for instance—was

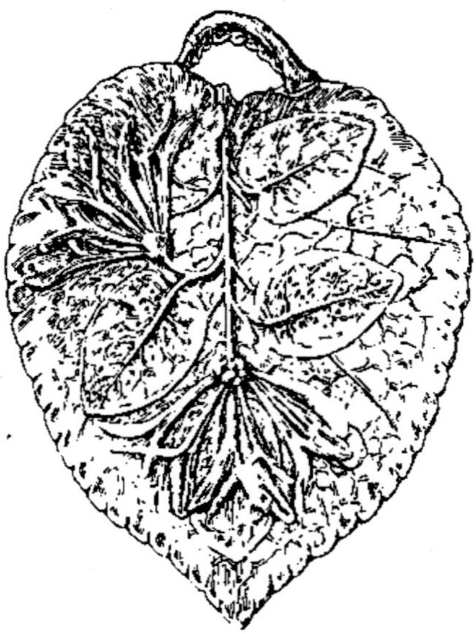

FIG. 50. TORTOISESHELL LEAF.—COLL. L. S.

transformed into a jug or a cup; the upper part, with its lozenge-shaped imbrications, received the yellow glaze they knew so well how to make rich and bright, while their dark green glaze seemed especially intended to reproduce the vivid colour of the pointed leaves ornamentally arranged underneath (Fig. 51). The same notions, applied to the reproduction of a melon resting on its leaf, inaugurated another style of ware. Treated in various ways, the pieces upon which this fruit was introduced all went by the name of melon-ware, and so were styled also the generality of pieces mottled green and yellow.

From the imitation of common fruits and vegetables the potters derived their most successful patterns.

Fig. 51. Pine-apple Jug.—Coll. L. S.

Cauliflower-ware was manufactured in enormous quantities, and in many sizes and shapes. Its novelty and originality remain striking even to our day. The potters took a just pride in the perfection of their cream-colour body and their green glaze. Nothing simpler could have been devised to bring out their quality and contrast them together. How well the one comes in to represent the flowers with their smooth emboss-ments and their thousands of minute dots, and the other to cover with a mellow and powerful colour the net-work of sunk and raised lines that veins the curled leaves! The execution is as simple and forcible as the idea. It has just the amount of conventional treatment that a work of art demands to become a "Type." There are

FIG. 52. CAULIFLOWER TEA-POT.—COLL. L. S.

many more pretentious pieces which have fewer claims to be spoken of in the same way (Fig. 52).

A French author says that he who creates a new proverb does more for the advancement of human wisdom than they who write exhaustive books; in the same way, a man who invents a new type might be said to do more towards improving the art of his time than another who achieves a skilful and elaborate work. This, we think, holds good with respect to the industrial artist who chances to hit upon an idea, so well calculated to please, that its successes will afford employment to a large number of his fellows. How many workmen in the Potteries were kept employed in reproducing the first cauliflower pieces, the happy thought of some unknown block cutter! The idea, as we have seen, was turned to all sorts of purposes, and for a time all the makers manufactured cauliflower ware with ever-increasing success.

Fancy, cramped a little by the requirements of table-ware, found an unlimited scope for its display in the merely ornamental articles that were already in demand; quaintly modelled by local artists, and made pleasant with the brightest hues of underglaze colour, all sorts of household and toy pieces were made; strange birds, curious animals, hippopotami and elephants, hanging vases bearing a large sunflower, which would have delighted the modern æsthete, flower vases for the decoration of the mantel-piece, even small figures, busts or medallions of the king and queen, and of the worthies of the day. We must also mention the wares made in imitation of Chinese porcelain; although they purport to be decorated with apple blossoms and mandarins, they are rather original fancies derived from a curious style imperfectly studied, than the actual copy of any particular piece. Upon them all the English hand is easily traceable; but, instead of being content with a mere imitation of the commonest productions of the East in the simple way that had at first been followed, *Whieldon* endeavoured to reproduce those which looked most complicated. Some tea-pots are perforated and cut all over the surface, exhibiting an unusual amount of ingenuity and skill, and must once have been considered marvels of workmanship. They are made in a double shell, the outer one being pierced according to a design of leaves and apple blossoms disposed for that purpose; this cutting out covers the shape with a sort of lace-work, very light in appearance, and the peculiar tints of English tortoiseshell-ware impart to the whole a look of originality which makes one forget that the piece was an imitation. Perforated tea-pots of the same description are also found in a dry red body. The effect produced by that outward piercing is at once so charming and surprising to one who does not comprehend how it can be executed, that we have seen the process revived many times at different places, and always given out as a fresh invention. We must not forget to mention the large two-handled cups which took the place of the discarded Tyg. In the improved household foreign wines had replaced the homely ale, and a light and handsome vessel had to be provided instead of the heavy posset pot. Those that have come down to us are remarkably well turned and finished; they were used as loving cups or wine-coolers; a climbing vine spreads its branches and tendrils all over the outer surface; to the stems, made by hand, leaves and bunches of grapes have been stuck at intervals. If any meaning is attached to the decoration, we may surmise that the time-honoured beer and spice

FIG. 53. TORTOISESHELL CUP.—COLL. L. S.

mixture was not to be brewed in this cup; at all events, the most fastidious man could be adequately gratified by possessing such a nicely made piece of bright earthenware, when he was debarred by his means of boasting of such luxuries as a silver or a china bowl.

Of all these, many identical replicas are still to be met with; it is to be borne in mind that as yet painting, which can indefinitely vary the aspect of the same piece, had not come to the potter's assistance; moulded shapes and raised decorations were alone resorted to, and the effect could merely be diversified by the stains of the mottled glazes (Fig. 53).

It is somewhat provoking, when we know most of the names of the tortoiseshell potters, to be unable to ascribe accurately to any of them the different specimens that we value and admire; no mark ever appears to help us, and none ever thought of following the practice of *Toft* by signing their best works. A piece of handiwork showing an individual taste, or a certain amount of skill, is always exceptionally valued in comparison with what has been done to a pattern. Hence it was that the old Slip dishes generally bore the name of the maker, who was proud to affix his signature to those unwonted proofs of his talent. Whether incomplete or imperfect, these works were unreservedly admired by the possessor, who, no doubt, had never seen them surpassed; and as most of them are perforated for suspension, we may suppose they were kept as desirable ornaments, and not intended to be put to any practical use. When, in course of time, the process of casting and moulding permitted the reproduction of the same piece by the score, the potter did not think it worth while to sign them any longer; it was only as a safeguard against imposition, and as a necessity of the trade, that, many years later, *Josiah Wedgwood* thought of marking with his name the productions of his manufactory. Artistic property was in no way protected, perhaps not even acknowledged; as soon as a model enjoyed a run of success, it was at once taken up by a crowd of imitators. *Whieldon* used to bury his imperfect pieces, lest they should be picked up and copied, but it was an ineffectual precaution after all, and his happiest novelties soon fell a prey to the plagiarist. Pirating other's ideas and shapes was considered almost legitimate; we know that later on many manufacturers thrived upon designs borrowed from *Wedgwood's* productions. The poor struggling potter, who could not keep a modeller, depended for his forms upon the assistance of his wealthier brethren, and took from him his best models, with or without his permission, in the same manner as a workman who in our days sets up in a small way of business on his own account, asks a neighbour for the loan of his blocks to make moulds from.

We can only distinguish the early pieces from those made long afterwards in the old moulds, by their being cast instead of pressed, and thereby being much thinner in the substance. Impressed in terra-cotta moulds, the ornaments are neater and sharper, the thick glaze is of a deeper tint, and the colours run more freely. Some are stamped with seals like the "Salt-glaze," and partly made by hand; all of them are "potted" with a skill and care often wanting in more modern productions.

The reliefs are often stamped on a black ground, or the whole piece is mottled with manganese; in these cases they were decorated with size gilding, or gold-leaf fixed with a hard varnish. It was only towards the end of the eighteenth century that the burning in of the gold was known in the Potteries. Imperfect as this mode of gilding may have been, yet it had one quality, it was transparent and mellow in colour, and looked certainly more like the Oriental gold than the burnished metal employed at a later period upon china; on most pieces it has now disappeared, or only faint traces remain of it in places.

Painting on cream-colour, which was soon to be so generally practised, was also introduced when the body had been made white enough to resemble china more closely. This whitening was obtained by the mixing of a small quantity of zaffre with the glaze; and this innovation, continued to our time, was due to *Aaron Wedgwood* and *William Littler*, who were also the first to glaze their ware by immersion. Certain proportions of the glaze, of the clay which composed the body of the pottery, and a small quantity of zaffre were mixed with water; in this liquid the vessels, when dry, were dipped, and absorbing the water, received a thick coating of the ground materials in suspension.

Shortly after this, *Enoch Booth* began the practice of firing his ware before dipping it; we accept this on the testimony of Shaw, noticing at the same time that firing in biscuit was practised by all the makers of Delft-ware.

Towards 1750, *R. and T. Baddeley*, of Shelton, made the first attempts at blue painting under the glaze, and the process was adopted by all the other potters.

Enamelling on cream-colour was successfully carried on at the same period by *Mrs. Warburton*, who is credited with having, in 1751, made the last improvement in earthenware bodies; she acquired a great celebrity for her painting, and until 1769 she enamelled for *Josiah Wedgwood.*

Another enamel painter was *Warner Edwards*, of Hanley; he not only worked himself, but supplied the trade with colours of his own making. He died in 1753.

When painting came into fashion, few trained hands could be obtained in the Potteries; many were sent for from Holland, where there was a superabundance of clever men; this may in some measure account for the small degree of originality noticeable on the painted pieces, when compared with those modelled and embossed according to the traditional style of the old English potter;

here we may incidentally remark that England was not the only country which borrowed her ceramic painters from abroad. In the records of the old Saint Lucas Guild, the Academy of Delft, to which the best faïence decorators were affiliated, many of the names inscribed as members, as far back as 1645, are those of foreigners who had come from France and Italy.

From this time pottery will lower itself into becoming the humble retainer of aristocratic porcelain; the body will try to ape the whiteness of its prototype, if not its transparency; blue painting will adopt the Worcester style; enamel decoration will emulate the works of Bow and Chelsea, and thus become a second-hand imitation of Oriental china. The lead-glaze and the smooth surface of the cream-colour were perfectly adapted to kiln painting, and this sort of decoration was at first fairly used, but as it could only by its cheapness compete with the china it was intended to replace, nothing of importance was ever attempted. A bright iron red was often used alone or relieved with a few touches of varied colours; Dutch landscapes or grotesque scenes were sometimes freely sketched, and groups of flowers were painted with bright enamels in a conventional manner. We give here (Fig. 54) the sketch of a loving cup, probably a presentation piece, enamelled in colours; on one side with a coat of arms, of which we have only been able to trace two of the quarterings: *Brete*, and *Pershall Bart.*, both families belonging to Staffordshire; and on the other side, with the monogram E. G., and the date 1770. However, as pieces of this sort generally belong to the second half of the eighteenth century, they hardly come within our scope, and we shall not linger on the subject; let it suffice to say that the style of

FIG. 54. CREAM-COLOUR TWO-HANDLED CUP.—COLL. L. S.

painting was gradually simplified, and the transition can easily be traced from the over-decorated pieces to the plain earthenware, merely edged with a brown or blue line, that was soon to come into fashion.

Meanwhile, the tortoiseshell-ware continued to be made, but the best efforts were brought to bear upon the new bodies, and the old style was losing some of its primitive character; the peculiar carving of blocks and "pitcher" moulds, and the engraving of ornament sunk in the hollow, were given up as being too slow and expensive, when the introduction of plaster of Paris gave facilities for casting moulds at a trifling cost, upon any model whatsoever, whether it was a piece of metal, china, or wood carving, little regard being paid to its fitness for reproduction in clay. Though the advantageous properties of plaster, its capability of taking an impression, and its porous substance which so rapidly absorbs the water, had been known for a long time previously in the Potteries, it was utilized but at a comparatively late period. A cream-colour tea-pot in the Liverpool Museum, with an embossed barley pattern, has an inscription scratched on the bottom, stating that this was the first tea-pot ever pressed, dated and signed "J. Hollingshead, 175..." The simple and well-adapted types created in the locality gave way to more ambitious models ordered from sculptors in London, who had never before thought of applying their talent to this new purpose. Tea-pots and jugs began to assume rustic and ultra-picturesque decorations, and to depart widely from geometrical and rational shapes.

We do not mean to say that fine and interesting pieces are not to be found amongst those resulting from this transformation of the Potter's style of modelling. The old man with short legs and ample waistcoat, whose cocked hat has been turned into use for a spout—the figure which constitutes the traditional Toby jug, and is the direct descendant of the Stone-ware Bellarmines—evinces a quaint spirit of originality (Fig. 55). Some groups were admirably modelled, and with a genuine sense of humour. The Sexton and

FIG. 55. TOBY JUG.—COLL. L. S.

the Parson going home arm-in-arm after a late supper; the Vicar asleep in his pulpit, while from underneath Moses vainly endeavours to prompt him with the next sentence of his sermon; the *Voyez* jug, with the huntsman and the milkmaid, of which Dr. Diamond has an example coloured with the most harmonious combinations of tortoiseshell glazes—these, and many others of the same kind, though of a date that brings them near to our own time, were still done with the old cream-colour, and stained with the softly-mottled glazes used by *Whieldon*. We possess a tea-pot in the shape of a head, which, although not of a very early period, is evidently cut by a working potter, and not modelled by an educated artist; it is remarkable for a feeling of originality, not at all lessened because the maker may have been actuated by the idea of emulating some antique vessel once seen and almost forgotten. The head, perhaps a local portrait, has the English periwig; the peculiar notching of the eyebrows and the character of the ornamentation exclude the supposition of it being a copy, but, as is the case with the Greek sculptures, an unconscious simplification in the rendering of natural forms changes into a work of high art that which, in a more realistic period, would only be vulgarity and grotesque fancy; it is in this respect nearer to the works of the ancients than many other pieces which can boast of being more faithful reproductions. All that we have just described is different, in our estimation, from the clumsy comicalities, made afterwards with white ware coloured on the surface, which are known by the name of Staffordshire figures.

In our judgment, an absolute line of demarcation separates the productions, however imperfect, of an art which kept steadfastly advancing in an original path, free from the intrusions of foreign notions, from those of a complex style, perhaps more correct, but which, after all, is only the fruit of studies often incomplete or ill-understood, and which admits of an admixture of totally irrelevant elements. When, for instance, we are pleased with the best pieces of English Salt-glaze or tortoiseshell, we never think of comparing them with any pieces belonging to another nation; they stand apart, and are to be taken as they are; they may at least be considered as the highest expression of a genuine taste, the development of which we can trace from its most uncouth and inexperienced early attempts. We feel a sense of disappointment and even of annoyance when we detect signs of a natural feeling having been perverted by extraneous teaching. Acanthus leaves are ill at ease on a Staffordshire tea-pot, and we are disheartened when we recognise upon the features of an otherwise coarse and vulgar figure a faint likeness to the Greek nose and the eye of Apollo. In one case we have a standard steadily advancing, in the other we have a decline savouring slightly of caricature.

But we are overstepping the bounds of our subject. It is not our purpose to follow the transformations of the Potter's art after the middle of the eighteenth century, the close of the epoch to which our investigations are limited. We must now briefly say that since that time earthenware pottery has thrived and flourished under the hands of innumerable skilful manufacturers, and has rapidly become the staple trade of all the English pottery-producing centres, from which it has spread to many places on the Continent, and even to the United States. A list of all those who had a hand in its improvement would be endless, as also would an enumeration of the places where it has been manufactured since 1750.

The limits we have thus imposed upon ourselves put beyond our range the admirable works of the greatest potter of England, *Josiah Wedgwood.* Of his innumerable achievements it would be unbecoming to speak in an inadequate manner, and his life must be read in the exhaustive books which have been devoted to his memory. For the same reason we are precluded from speaking of the earthenware of Liverpool, where almost all descriptions of Pottery were manufactured; of the cream-colour of Leeds, which equalled, if it did not surpass, the finest ware previously made at any other place; and of a host of Potters established all over the kingdom, whose names are mentioned and productions described in the works written on the subject. Many interesting discoveries must be passed over. We should like to relate how the transfer of a black print to the surface of a glazed piece gave rise to a new mode of decoration; how, shortly afterwards, under-glaze printing superseded painting in blue, and a bright and complicated pattern being thus obtainable at a small cost, a revolution was accomplished in the decoration of earthenware; but, however enticing the subject, we cannot attempt to treat of it here.

Our account has come to an end; the old English Potter, with his quaint ways, is replaced by the educated manufacturer with eclectic taste; but let us remember that we owe much to the intelligence and energy with which his modest forerunners prepared the way for the excellence now attained. If this imperfect essay helps to bring to light their merits and originality; if it can be accepted as a tribute to the memory of these neglected workmen and artists, who in their secluded pot works were once exerting their ingenuity, and who bequeathed to us the fruits of their labours, the writer's most earnest hopes will have been realised, and his effort will not have been made in vain.

APPENDIX.

FOREIGN IMITATIONS OF ENGLISH EARTHENWARE.

Opinion entertained in France on English Flint Ware towards the end of the last Century.—Emigration of English Operatives.—"Terre d'Angleterre" manufactured at Paris.—Edme Saladin, of St. Omer.—Peterinck, of Tournay. The Brothers Boch, of Septfontaine and Longwy.—Charles Bayard, of Bellevue.—Shaw, at Montereau. Desseaux de Romilly and Asselineau Grammont, of Orleans.—The Moulins, of Apt.—Ch. and J. Leigh, at Douai.—Lanfrey, at Niderviller.—Potter, Prince of Wales Works, at Paris.—Ollivier and Despres, at Paris.—Royal Manufactories of Sevres and Buen-Retiro.—De Bettignies, of St. Amand.—Pierre Senly, of Nevers; Vavasseur, of Rouen.—Francis Warburton, at La Charite sur Loire.—Arend de Haak, of Delft.

APPENDIX.

FOREIGN IMITATIONS OF ENGLISH EARTHENWARE.

SINCE we did not omit to render to the foreigner such credit as is due to him for the importation of many new kinds of processes which at one time had benefited the potting trade of England and assisted its development, it is but fair that we should also mention the many instances of Englishmen settling abroad for the purpose of establishing the English manufacture; it is almost a duty to relate, however briefly, when and where they settled, bringing with them the secrets of making a new sort of earthenware, which answered better than any other the wants of the time, and in so doing to assert to what an extent the Continent remains indebted to our potters. We shall endeavour to show in what follows that, if much had been once borrowed, much has been given in return, and the debt can now be considered as cancelled and paid in full.

So much was the English "faïence" admired and sought after during the eighteenth century, that the French government had thought it prudent to check the earliest attempts of its importation, first by taxing it with an almost prohibitory duty, and finally by striking it with absolute prohibition. To that effect were successively enacted the "décrèts" of 1740, 1749, and 1785; but in the succeeding year, 1786, the policy was reversed, and in accordance with the liberal movement which was beginning to shatter all the old institutions, protection was completely abandoned; henceforth the English ware was to be admitted on payment of a small duty of twelve per cent. It is most interesting to read the protestations in which the whole trade vented their grievances on the occasion of these new tariffs. They state in the most bitter terms that competition is no longer possible for the home manufacture. And indeed to the facility given to importation of foreign articles was afterwards attributed the closing of the factories of Rouen, Nevers, as well as of the other potting centres, culminating in the utter ruin of that branch of French industry.

To describe the opinion entertained in France upon the merits of the imported ware, we cannot do better than quote the following paragraph, extracted from one of the Ceramic Essays of the Chemist *Fourmy*. In his "Memoire sur les Hygiocèrames," presented to the French Academy in 1801, he says: "While faïence kept labouring under the sway of ancient routine, adhering to its coarse and vulgar shapes, and porcelain was trammelled with all the drawbacks resulting from its want of ductility and great vitrification, neither of them attempting to indulge in any freedom or refresh their old-fashioned style, English earthenware, unfettered with any of these difficulties, offered to the appreciation of the consumer new and elegant shapes, all the more seducing that they were accompanied with an unwonted lightness. How could it have been possible to resist admiring so charming a novelty, especially when it possessed besides, and as a further recommendation, the great merit of cheapness."

We shall now briefly record the names of the most important places where this manufacture was first introduced, as the first materials brought together towards a history, still to be written, of the English potters who successfully established their trade in distant countries, where very different sorts of wares had for centuries remained unrivalled. We have met with the names of very few who had previously made a mark amongst their countrymen, but one may easily surmise that it could not have been the well-known manufacturer who, generally successful in his speculations, would have left his home to hazard his fortunes abroad; this was rather to be expected of some obscure manager or workman, who, however skilled and thoroughly expert in all the branches of the art, and boasting of a knowledge acquired from the most accredited masters, could not, perhaps for want of capital or other causes, come to the front amongst his own people. To modest operatives may thus be traced the origin of such celebrated manufactories as those of Montereau, Longwy, Sarreguemines, Bordeaux, and a host of minor ones which started everywhere on the foreign principles, not only making the new ware according to the fashion practised in England, but also on the example of the British manufactories, being managed in a more business like manner. Capital was largely and judiciously invested, extensive and suitable premises were erected, science and machinery were called to the assistance of the practical potter, and the best artists were commissioned to supply models answering a more refined taste. In this manner were created the important manufactories which were destined to absorb, in their increasing prosperity, all the small pot works with which France abounded.

Taking by order of dates the names recorded in the industrial history of France, we find one *Edme* directing the "Manufacture Royale d'Angleterre," in Paris, at a period which corresponds to the last improvements in cream-colour by *Whieldon*, and long before the importation of *Wedgwood's* Queen's Ware. A guide book of Paris, published in 1745, tells us that it was situated in the Rue de Charenton, and table ware was especially manufactured there. Early as this date may appear, we must however bear in mind that *Ralph Shaw* had left Burslem with all his family for the purpose of settling abroad more than ten years previously. So far documents are wanting to show whether he had any hand in the establishment of that "Manufacture d'Angleterre," but that much may be surmised, as we lose traces of him until he reappears at Montereau in 1775.

Towards the middle of the eighteenth century, the "Terre d'Angleterre" manufactured in Paris was much valued. Several pieces of it are described in the inventory of the Chateau of Versailles, and the Duke of Aumont possessed two fine vases with bronze mountings, which at his sale fetched the sum of 300 livres.

Saladin, of Saint Omer, received, in 1745, letters patent to make faïence after the manner of Holland, and Stone-ware imitating that of England. We must remark here that the name of "Grés Anglais" was generally applied in France to the English flint-ware.

Peterinck, of Tournay, had engaged so many workmen to come over from England, that in 1759 the town council decided that an English Jesuit should be sent for at the expense of the town, to instruct and convert these workmen and their families to the Catholic religion. They were granted many privileges; one of them named Phœnix was for many years freed from paying any taxes.

The brothers *Boch*, after some abortive trials in France, began at Septfontaine, in Luxembourg, an important manufacture of "Faïence-fine," or cream-colour, towards the year 1767, and later on added to their establishment that of Longwy, both of which are still prospering in the hands of the same family.

Charles Bayard, of Bellevue, near Toul, obtained for his works, in 1772, the title of "Royal Manufactory," as a reward for his successful production of fine ware of white pipe clay. This, imitated in several places, became soon the staple trade of the province; there were made those dinner services and glazed ornaments, as well as those figures in white biscuit, so widely known and appreciated under the name of "Terre de Lorraine."

Shaw, and his partner, *William Clark*, of Newcastle, after having experimented at Lille and other places, settled at Montereau to manufacture English earthenware; and two ordinances, dated 1775, granted to the company several privileges, besides which they were for many years in receipt of an annual subsidy of 1,200 francs. A branch of the same factory was subsequently established at Creil, and both branches have continued to prosper and increase up to the present day.

Desseaux de Romilly obtained for his factory at Orleans a privilege for making a faïence of purified white earth, or cream-colour, and at the same time *Asselineau Grammont*, also of Orleans, was turning out various sorts of wares of coloured bodies, or marbled in imitation of English ware.

The *Moulins*, at Apt, in Provence, had towards the same period brought that same process of marbling on cream-colour to the highest degree of perfection, this style of decoration having probably been spread all over France by the workmen who had at first practised it in the northern provinces. The persecution directed in England against the Roman Catholics, which began in 1778, and culminated in the Gordon riots in 1780, resulted in a numerous emigration of English operatives, who had to take refuge on the Continent, and finding there permanent employment in the factories, vulgarised the ways and uses of the trade of their own country.

Amongst those who settled in the north we shall mention *Charles* and *Jacques Leigh*, who set up an important manufactory at Douai, where, in partnership with *Houzé de l'Aulnoy*, they were, towards 1780, making delicate snuff boxes, dainty little pieces of perforated cream-colour and agate ware, as well as a large quantity of table ware and ornamental articles. This decoration by marbling in clay acclimatized itself in the province, where it went by the name of "gaïolé," a local term for motley. Following up all the practices of the English potters, they stamped their ware with their name impressed in the clay, and it is not uncommon to find their pieces bearing the name of *Leigh & Cie.*

At Niedervillier the fabrication of stanniferous faïence was abandoned in 1785, to be superseded by that of flint-ware, under the management of *Lanfrey*, who advertises in the "Tableau du Commerce" his English earthenware, which, he says, "is for form, colour, and hardness, quite equal to that of England."

Potter, also an Englishman, established in 1789 a factory in the Rue de Crussol, at Paris, which he called the "Prince of Wales Works," and claimed a privilege for having been the first to practise in France decoration by transfer printing. Joseph Mayer, in his history of the Liverpool Potteries, says that an engraver named *Abbey*, who had served his time with *Sadler*, went to Paris for the purpose of teaching the art of engraving and transferring the prints on earthenware. We feel inclined to think that it was in connection with the enterprise mentioned above, though positive proofs are still wanting. *Potter* signed his ware with his full name stencilled underneath.

To *Ollivier*, Rue de la Roquette, at Paris, was granted a patent in 1791, for his imitations of *Wedgwood* ware, black and cane bodies, and also for his reproductions of white and blue jasper for medallions and buttons. In the year 1797, *Desprès* is spoken of as manufacturing the same articles with great ability, at his works of the Rue de Lancry. It is well known that the Royal Manufactory of Sèvres had already tried to imitate with white and blue porcelain the much admired cameos and plaques of Wedgwood jasper, and that they were frequently introduced in the decoration of the costly furniture of the period. At Buen-Retiro white and blue cameos were also made, and Charles IV. had a whole room decorated with them, in the part of the Escurial erected during his reign.

A glance at the catalogues of the products of French factories, published at the end of the last century, will convince us of the change undergone by the public taste. For instance, in the list of articles made and sold at St. Amand by *De Bettignies*, nothing is mentioned but what is made "façon Anglaise."

Small factories sprung up at that time in every direction, and in the once prosperous towns where the now discarded faïence had been for so long the staple trade of the place, ineffectual attempts were made to cope against a ruinous competition, by introducing the new fashioned ware by the side of the lingering old one. Thus we find the names of *Pierre Senly*, at Nevers, in the year 1795, and of *Vavasseur*, at Rouen, 1788, connected with some attempts at producing English earthenware; but, as in the case of La Charité sur Loire, where *Francis Warburton*, of Hot-lane, set up a factory, which from 1802 to 1812 was making cream-colour and Egyptian black basalt, success does not seem to have attended their speculation. The new ware could not thrive on old grounds; there the new notions, hampered by the old routine, could not develop themselves, the ruin could not be averted, and the trade departed from those places to be transferred to the rising localities where the spirit of enterprise had started anew upon a completely fresh track.

This hasty nomenclature would have to be extended far beyond our present purpose, were we to mention the many instances of importation of the English process on the Continent. In Sweden, Spain, Italy, and Germany, they were numerous. We shall merely refer the reader to the local histories in which they are recorded. Yet we cannot omit to recall the striking fact of the downfall of Delft, a town where potting was once so flourishing that the place could boast of being the largest centre of production in the whole world. Towards the end of the last century the trade was dwindling away with rapidity, nearly all its establishments had been closed. In the Staffordshire Potteries, *Turner*, of Lane End, was manufacturing large quantities of table ware expressly for the Dutch market, and the last of the painters, still remaining at Delft, found a precarious living in decorating those services in the questionable style then prevailing in Holland. Specimens are still commonly met with, mostly decorated with the portrait of William of Orange, outlined in black with a pen and rudely coloured over with red, yellow, and green. *Arend de Haak* thought he could retain something of what had been the source of riches in his town, by transforming his factory, and hoped that by employing English workmen he should be able to compete with the fashionable importation. But his attempts, as well as those of some of his countrymen, were doomed to fail; no efforts could delay the ruin of the old fabrics, nor stop the rising fortunes of the new ones.

More causes than one may account for the revolution which was thus accomplished in the potting trade; we must acknowledge that it is not altogether to the appearance of English ware upon the Continental markets that it may be attributed. A great reason for the change in the public taste can be traced to the facility with which the more handsome and valuable translucent porcelain began to be produced in Europe, and substituted its elegant and refined material for the heavy and ponderous substance of the stanniferous faïence. However, no one can fail to be astonished at the rapidity with which the flint ware, glazed with lead, invented by the old Staffordshire potter, supplanted in France and other countries, whether under the name of Terre de pipe, Faïence fine, Grès Anglais, or Caïlloutage, the many products which had found their glorious origin on the soil. In the same manner was transformed the process of decoration; and the new mode of decorating by transfer printing, which is every day used more and more extensively, is an indirect homage rendered to the ingenuity of the invention of *Sadler & Green*, of Liverpool. Indeed, we go so far as to say that, actuated by a feeling akin to that which prompts man to revere and worship the memory of his ancestors and all that has been handed down to him from them (if such a feeling was still lingering in our age), all of us who are connected with pottery, either as manufacturers, collectors, or artisans, should enshrine in our best cabinet and treasure as inestimable relics, the works of the early English potter, from which are undoubtedly derived our modern fabrics.

GENERAL INDEX.

ENGLISH ART IN 1884. Containing about Three Hundred and Fifty Sketches, many of them by the artists themselves, and Fourteen Photogravure Plates of Pictures in the Royal Academy, the Grosvenor Gallery, the Societies of Painters in Water-Colors, and the Royal Institute of Painters in Oils of 1884. With Descriptive Text by HENRY BLACKBURN. Large 4to. Cloth, gilt top, $12.00.

ARTISTS AT HOME. Consisting of a Series of Photo-Engravings of the leading English Painters and Sculptors of the Day, in their Studios or in their Homes. Sold only by subscription.

The artists whose portraits and studios have been reproduced are as follows: Sir F. LEIGHTON, President of the Royal Academy; ALMA-TADEMA, L., R. A.; BARLOW, T. O., R. A.; BOEHM, J. E., R. A.; CALDERON, P. H., R. A.; COUSINS, S., Hon. Retired R. A.; DICKSEE, F., A. R. A.; GILBERT, Sir J., R. A.; LAWSON, C. A.; MACBETH, R. W., A. R. A.; MACWHIRTER, J., A. R. A.; MARSHALL, W. C., R. A.; MILLAIS, J. E., R. A.; PETTIE, J., R. A.; POYNTER, E. J., R. A.; PRINSEP, V. C., A. R. A.; REDGRAVE, RICHARD, Hon. Retired R. A.; RIVIERE, BRITON, R. A.; STONE, MARCUS, A. R. A.; STOREY, G. A., A. R. A.; THORNYCROFT, W. H., A. R. A.; WATTS, G. F., R. A.; WEBSTER, T., Hon. Retired R. A.; YEAMES, W. F., R. A.; also the Right Hon. W. E. GLADSTONE, M. P., Professor of Ancient History to the Royal Academy, in his study.

The size of the work is Imperial 4to, 5 + 95 pages. The text and plates are printed on the finest paper. An edition of five hundred copies only has been struck off for the American market. The present price of the work is $15.00, the publishers reserving the right to advance the price at any time.

HOURS WITH ART AND ARTISTS. By G. W. SHELDON. With Twelve Engravings on Steel, and Eighty-nine Illustrations on Wood. Imperial 4to. Cloth, extra gilt, $7.50.

The principal artists represented in this book are Bouguereau, Rosa Bonheur, Doré, Frère, Boughton, Munkacsy, Detaille, De Neuville, Fortuny, Millais, Corot, Millet, Gérôme, Couture, Zamacois, Vibert, Meissonnier, Birket Foster, Landelle, Toulmouche, Bridgman, Beckwith, Chase, Swain Gifford, Colman, Winslow Homer, Quartley, Wyatt Eaton, Thayer, and Moran, the illustrations being in nearly every case figure-subjects. Many of the pictures are full-page, and all are engraved and printed in the best manner.

THE TURNER GALLERY. A Series of One Hundred and Twenty Engravings on Steel, from the Works of J. M. W. TURNER, R. A. In two folio volumes. Published by subscription. Half morocco, $32.00; full morocco, $36.00.

Each plate is accompanied by historical and critical remarks, compiled from authentic sources, so that the whole affords a most instructive guide to the study of Turner's unrivaled pictures.

OUR NATIVE LAND; OR, GLANCES AT AMERICAN SCENERY AND PLACES. With Sketches of Life and Adventure. With 336 Illustrations. Imperial 8vo. Cloth, $5.50; gilt edges, $6.00; morocco, $12.00. Sold by subscription.

REPUBLICAN COURT; OR, AMERICAN SOCIETY IN THE DAYS OF WASHINGTON. By R. W. GRISWOLD. Enlarged edition, with additional portraits. Imperial 8vo. French morocco, $7.50.